⚖ NOLO   The Trusted Name
(but don't take our word for it)

"In Nolo you can trust."

THE NEW YORK TIMES

"Nolo is always there in a jam as the nation's premier publisher of do-it-yourself legal books."

NEWSWEEK

"Nolo publications…guide people simply through the how, when, where and why of the law."

THE WASHINGTON POST

"[Nolo's]…material is developed by experienced attorneys who have a knack for making complicated material accessible."

LIBRARY JOURNAL

"When it comes to self-help legal stuff, nobody does a better job than Nolo…"

USA TODAY

"The most prominent U.S. publisher of self-help legal aids."

TIME MAGAZINE

"Nolo is a pioneer in both consumer and business self-help books and software."

LOS ANGELES TIMES

Selling Your House

Nolo's Essential Guide

Ilona Bray, J.D.

FIRST EDITION   JANUARY 2015

Editor   KATHLEEN MICHON

Cover Design   SUSAN PUTNEY

Proofreading   ROBERT WELLS

Index   SONGBIRD INDEXING SERVICES

Printing   BANG PRINTING

Bray, Ilona M., 1962-
  Selling your house : Nolo's essential guide / Ilona Bray, J.D. -- First edition.
      pages cm
  Includes index.
  ISBN 978-1-4133-2120-3 (pbk.) -- ISBN 978-1-4133-2121-0 (epub ebook)
  1. House selling--United States. 2. Residential real estate--United States. I. Title.
  HD259.B733 2015
  643'.120973--dc23

                       2014038086

This book covers only United States law, unless it specifically states otherwise.

Please note

We believe accurate, plain-English legal information should help you
solve many of your own legal problems. But this text is not a substitute
for personalized advice from a knowledgeable lawyer. If you want the
help of a trained professional—and we'll always point out situations
in which we think that's a good idea—consult an attorney licensed to
practice in your state.

Acknowledgments

Is there any one person in the United States who can fully and accurately describe everything involved in selling a house? Doubtful. The process involves a mix of wisdom and skills: marketing, finance, law, negotiation, interior decorating, and much more. And just when you think you know a thing or two, the real estate or financial market changes.

That's why, in preparing this book, we drew on numerous experienced professionals for tips and guidance, including:

- Nancy Atwood, Broker and District Manager with NRT in Framingham, Massachusetts
- Katy Ayer, CPA with Five Cities CPAs in Arroyo Grande, California (www.5citiescpas.com/index.php)
- George Devine, licensed real estate broker in San Francisco and author and educator in the real estate field
- Marjo Diehl, loan agent and Vice President with RPM Mortgage, Inc., in Alamo, California (www.rpm-mtg.com)
- Kenneth Goldstein, attorney with Goldstein & Herndon, LLP, in Brookline, Massachusetts (www.brooklinelaw.com)
- Joel G. Kinney, Founder at Fort Point Legal in Boston, Massachusetts
- Richard Leshnower, an attorney practicing in the state of New York
- Mark Nash, Illinois real estate agent and author of *1001 Tips for Buying and Selling a Home*
- Carol Neil, independent broker and Realtor in Berkeley, California (www.carolneil.com)
- Greg Nino, RE/MAX Realtor in Houston, Texas (www.everdayhoustonhomes.com)
- Janet Portman, attorney, author, Nolo editor, and syndicated columnist
- Amy Robeson, real estate broker with Pacific Union in Berkeley and Oakland, California (www.amyrobeson.com)
- Paul A. Rude, professional inspector and owner of Summer Street Inspections, based in Berkeley, California (www.summerinspect.com)

- Ira Serkes, agent with Pacific Union in Berkeley, California, and coauthor of Nolo's *How to Buy a House in California* (www.berkeleyhomes.com)
- Daniel Stea, broker/owner/attorney at Stea Realty Group, in Berkeley, California (www.stearealtygroup.com)
- Ngaire Taylor, Loan Officer with Eagle Home Mortgage in Lynnwood, Washington (www.eaglehomemortgage.com), and
- Patricia and David Wangsness, Realtors with Coldwell Banker Bain Associates in Bellevue, Washington (www.wangsnessconnections.com).

A number of home sellers were also generous enough to tell us about their experiences and let us publish their accounts, including Cathy Caputo, Wren Conroy, Linda Garey, Carter Wall, Kyung Yu, and others who wished to remain anonymous.

Here at Nolo, special thanks go to Legal Editor Kathleen Michon, who provided not only masterful editing but expert advice on consumer credit and secured transaction matters; Acquisitions Editor Marcia Stewart, who made sure this book became a possibility and offered numerous substantive ideas and additions; former editor Alayna Schroeder, who provided some of the research and material that eventually found its way into this book; and Nolo's Production Department, including Jaleh Doane, and Susan Putney, who made the final version look great.

About the Author

Ilona Bray is an author and legal editor at Nolo, specializing in real estate, immigration law, and nonprofit fundraising. She is a coauthor of *Nolo's Essential Guide to Buying Your First Home*, *First-Time Landlord: Your Guide to Renting Out a Single-Family Home*, and numerous other top-selling books. Bray also blogs on Nolo's Real Estate Tips for Home Buyers and Sellers.

Bray's working background includes solo practice, nonprofit, and corporate stints, as well as long periods of volunteering, including an internship at Amnesty International's main legal office in London. She received an A.B. from Bryn Mawr College and her law degree and a master's degree in East Asian (Chinese) Studies from the University of Washington.

Table of Contents

Introduction:
What's Ahead in Selling Your House

D o you need a book to help you sell your home? In some markets in the United States today, homes practically seem to sell themselves. And, you'll likely have a real estate agent by your side, offering experience and advice, and handling much of the legwork.

Nevertheless, there are ample compelling reasons to educate yourself on the process—ideally before calling in an agent and putting your home on the market. Big dollars are at stake in this transaction (as if you hadn't noticed). Sellers whose mental energies are elsewhere risk either disregarding the advice of a wise agent or overlooking the failings of a mediocre one—perhaps resulting in a lower home sale price than was possible. (And a few sellers will decide that their best course of action is to go without an agent, in which case some advance study will be crucial.)

With the help of this book you can figure out important things, like what to do first after deciding to sell your home, what to look for in and expect from a real estate agent, how to get top dollar for your home, how the law protects you (and what it requires of you) when you enter into a purchase agreement with a buyer, and much more. We'll discuss all these matters, with the help of real estate agents and home sellers who have contributed tips and stories from the real estate trenches.

But first, let's look at the big picture: the key steps in selling your home. Review these before you dive into the process—you'll learn what to expect, and see how the different pieces fit together.

- **Assess your house's current condition.** Taking a hard look at the condition of your home will give you a heads up on repair needs, identify key selling points (and the opposite), and inform your pricing. You can do a preliminary evaluation yourself (see Chapter 1) and/or bring in an outside professional to ferret out issues you may not have the expertise to spot (Chapter 3).

- **Find the best real estate agent, attorney, and possibly tax pro to assist you.** We will assume that, like most home sellers, you'll have an agent by your side. The agent provides a second set of eyes, may suggest needed repairs or improvements, will help strategize about long-term issues such as the best time to put the place on the market, perform market analysis to come up with a list price, help you sort through offers, negotiate with buyers, and make sure the many tasks necessary for the deal to close get done. Either the agent or an attorney may help you draft or negotiate the sales contract. A tax professional may also be a good person to bring onto your team, particularly in complex financial situations or if your profits might exceed the IRS capital gains tax exclusion ($250,000 for individuals, $500,000 for married couples filing jointly). Of course, you'll want to take the time to interview a few agents or other professionals and choose ones who are well-respected and suit your needs (discussed in Chapter 2). We'll also address the alternative of selling without the help of an agent, called selling by owner or FSBO (see Chapter 11).

- **Perform repairs and improvements.** You'll need to decide which problems to fix and which to leave alone (you'll have to disclose them to the buyer, however) and what other improvements will help sell your home or bring in a higher price. Home projects are famous for taking longer and costing more than expected. You'll want to get going on the repair needs that you, your inspector, and your real estate agent identify as priorities as soon as your time and budget allows. See Chapters 3 and 5 for further guidance on this part of the process.

- **Fill out a written disclosure report.** Complying with your legal obligation (in the majority of U.S. states) to give sellers a fully completed document explaining the home's physical features and their condition (highlighting any defects) should be done just before you put the house on the market. By then, you may have eliminated some problems through repairs. Nevertheless, it's a task that will require some serious attention, as described in Chapter 4.

- **Declutter, clean, and perhaps stage the house.** Having dealt with what's under the hood, it's time to make your home look its best. Of course, depending on how much stuff is in your home now, doing the necessary sorting, organizing, selling things at a garage sale, on eBay, or on Craigslist, and donating the leftovers may take months. See Chapter 5 for tips on this.
- **Take photos and videos.** Your agent will likely arrange for photos and videos. A good agent will hire a pro for this. It will need to be carefully timed, so that your house is looking its best and you'll have the images ready for advertising materials and the house's website or Web pages on your broker's site. This is further covered in Chapter 7, which discusses marketing your home.
- **Set a list price.** You may already have an approximate (or wished-for) price in your head. Don't get locked into your thinking on that quite yet, however. It's best to finalize your list price after you and your agent have seen what the house looks like after you've fixed and dressed it up a bit and—if you're in a rapidly changing market—have evaluated the comparable homes that sold within the previous few weeks. You'll announce the list price at the same time you announce that the home is for sale. Chapter 6 covers choosing a list price.
- **Announce that the home is for sale.** With your agent's help, the house will be advertised for sale on the Multiple Listing Service (the "MLS," an online database used by real estate agents), as well as on the agent's website and probably other real estate sites. Some sellers even use Craigslist! (This step is also covered in Chapter 7, concerning marketing.) Things will start moving quickly at this point. As soon as the house is announced for sale, the public will assume that it will be available for individual showings.
- **Hold a broker's open house.** Have you noticed "Open House" signs at odd times, such as on a Thursday afternoon? Most likely this is a "brokers' open," in which agents troop out and get an advance look at what will be publicly shown the following Sunday. These can be raucous affairs, with agents

passing judgments, comparing notes, and—with any luck—contacting their home-buying clients to say, "Hey, I've found a great one for you." (Further discussion in Chapter 7.)

- **Hold an open house.** Agents argue endlessly about whether Sunday open houses really bring in serious buyers, but public showings remain an important part of the process of getting your home seen and talked about. Besides, plenty of buyers have walked into an open house and fallen in love. Chapter 7 will discuss how to hold an open house.

- **Watch the offers roll in!** Hopefully, anyway. Receiving even one offer may take weeks, if you're in a slow market—or you may be immediately inundated with competing offers from eager buyers, as occurs in many areas of the U.S. today. Evaluating the strength of these offers is a critical part of the process, described in Chapter 8. You may need to counteroffer or negotiate before you agree to accept one particular offer.

- **Sign a sales contract.** Once you've chosen and accepted an offer, you'll need to set that forth in a formal, written, legally binding document. Your buyer may have done most of the work for you, by filling out a standard form. How to understand what that document means and negotiate over some of the finer points is covered in Chapter 9.

- **Get through escrow.** At least a few weeks will likely pass between the signing of the sales contract and the scheduled closing of the deal. Chapter 10 will help you understand your obligations during this period and deal with any surprises.

- **Close the deal.** The finalizing of your home sale is typically more work for the buyer than the seller. After all, it's the buyer who needs to worry about paying for the place. Nevertheless, Chapter 10 will acquaint you with your obligations at this point, including how to deal with last-minute difficulties, such as the buyer reneging on the deal.

CAUTION
This book assumes your home sale will be straightforward.
Matters could get more complicated if, for instance, siblings are working together to sell the home of an aging parent, or you are selling a vacation home. Such circumstances may add steps to the usual process, such as family meetings or long-distance travel. We'll highlight such issues in some instances, but won't deal with them in detail.

Get Updates, Checklists, Calculators, and More at Nolo.com

You can find the online companion page to this book at:

www.nolo.com/back-of-book/SELL.html

There you will find important updates to the law; podcasts; links to mortgage calculators, Nolo's real estate blog, and online home-selling articles; downloadable home-selling checklists; and more.

Other Helpful Real Estate Books by Nolo

If you are selling your home, you may also be buying one. Or, if push comes to shove and you can't sell your home, you may think about renting it out. Nolo has several books that can assist you with these tasks, as well as a book specific to selling FSBO in California.

- *For Sale by Owner in California*, by George Devine.
- *Nolo's Essential Guide to Buying Your First Home* (despite the title, it's useful to all home buyers), by Ilona Bray, Alayna Schroeder, and Marcia Stewart.
- *First-Time Landlord: Your Guide to Renting Out a Single-Family Home*, by Ilona Bray, Janet Portman, and Marcia Stewart.

To check out Nolo's full library of real estate books, see the "Real Estate" section of the Nolo store on www.nolo.com, or call Nolo at 800-728-3555.

First Steps: What You Can Do *Now* to Get Ready to Sell

How soon are you hoping to sell your home? Depending on your own readiness to move and what shape your house is in, it's ideal—though not absolutely necessary—to start planning this major life event several months in advance. Once you hire an agent, there will be lots to do to get your home ready for sale. But even before you get to that point, there are steps you can take, and things to start thinking about, to get a head start.

This chapter will cover some of the things you can do yourself as well as some of the big issues to consider before jumping into the process, including:

- evaluating your home's condition and identifying issues that you might want to address right away
- becoming aware of your house's strong points, for marketing purposes
- developing a strategic goal for when would be best to put your house on the market
- looking at other homes for sale in your area, for comparison purposes, and
- budgeting for the typical costs of sale.

Chapter 2 will lead you through the important process of choosing an agent.

No Need to Wait: Start Fixing and Decluttering!

Your house is beautiful! Well, as long as you don't look too hard at that spot on the carpet where the baby spilled pureed beets, or the marks by the door where the dog scratches to go out, or the pile of magazines that's turning into its own piece of furniture … you get the idea. No matter how clean and tidy you are, your house is probably not as market-ready as you'd thought or hoped. If you're anything like the average home seller, you've been in your home for about nine years. (Source: National Association of Realtors 2013 *Profile of Home Buyers and Sellers*.) A lot can happen to a place, and a lot of stuff can pile up, in that amount of time. The more you've put off dealing with it, the sooner you should get going.

"Two months is an ideal amount of prep time once you get an agent involved," says Carol Neil, a Berkeley-based broker with over 30 years' experience. "Some houses don't need that much time, and a good agent can whip things into gear in a matter of days—but I've also worked with sellers for over a year to get the place ready. The houses that tend to need the most prep are the ones that the seller has lived in for the longest time. They've lived with the problems for years, and don't see them."

Given the work involved in getting your home ready for market, you might want to dive in before you've chosen an agent. (If you're not inclined to start this on your own, don't worry. A good agent will help you with this process.)

When prospective buyers come along, they'll likely be scrutinizing your home's condition. Obvious issues that a nonprofessional could pick out, such as the beet stains and dog scratches mentioned above, can make any home harder to sell, or lower its value. Other issues that buyers tend to notice right away include doors that don't close well, bad smells, sloping or stained floors, curling linoleum, cracks in the walls and ceiling or tiles, and cracks or scratches on any cabinet or countertop finishes.

CAUTION

"Deferred maintenance" can be a red flag for buyers. Little problems with a house are widely viewed as indicators that the owner doesn't take good care of the place. Even if the buyers don't notice this issue themselves, their agents may raise it with them. They'll start looking for larger, looming problems you may have also ignored.

The state of your local market does play a major role in how much fixing up you ultimately need to do, however. According to California Realtor Ira Serkes, "The Berkeley market has become so hot that unless there's a health and safety issue, our philosophy is to provide extensive disclosures, reports, and contractor estimates to the buyers before they write their offer rather than actually doing the work. As long as buyers know what they're getting into, their eagerness to buy the home means they generally view the repair needs as no big deal." And, adds California Realtor Amy Robeson, "You wouldn't want to miss the peak selling season because you got overwhelmed by all the work that could be done."

So, until you've met with an agent, you might want to focus on minimal repairs only—those that are eyesores and easily fixed for around $50 or less, such as a missing cabinet knob or wires hanging from the wall from an old security system. But it's worth starting a list of other issues that you notice, for you and your agent to go over later. Chapter 3 will guide you further along in this process, and also discuss the possibility of hiring a professional to preinspect your house.

It's never too early to get a head start on decluttering, however— in other words, minimizing the amount of stuff taking up space in your house. This will be important in order to make your house look its best, possibly prepare it for staging by a professional, and of course reduce the volume that you must box up and move to your next abode. How long this process will take may depend on your relationship to material objects as well as on how badly you need the money that could be earned by selling off items one by one.

L esson learned the hard way **I should have donated more from the outset.** Karina explains, "Having lived through the Great Depression, I know I have trouble throwing anything away. On top of that, my husband and I were preparing to move into assisted living, so there was the added trauma of parting with a lifetime of memories. I must have spent two years going back and forth to consignment shops, holding garage sales, advertising on Craigslist, sending items to my children, and so on. It was probably the world's longest moving process, thoroughly exhausting—and now I hardly miss any of the things I parted with."

Where to Sell Your Stuff

No need to jump online right away. Local consignment, used book, clothing, and vintage or antique stores can be the most lucrative places to sell your possessions. Or if you're downsizing, talk to an estate sale specialist. Your next stops might be Craigslist (which lets you sell items one by one) and eBay (where you'll need to register as a "seller").

A garage sale can work if your house is well located, but can also be a huge waste of time. In fact, your goods might be more valuable as tax deductions, after donating them to charity.

You might also check out these online possibilities:

- **Etsy.com.** Best known as a crafts site, you can also sell vintage clothing, jewelry, and other items here. (The objects must be 20 years old or older.)
- **Bookscouter.com.** Here, you can enter a book's ISBN number and learn which online book buyer is paying the most for it. Also look into Half.com (an eBay company), popular for selling used books.
- **Thredup.com.** This site lets you order a "Clean Out Bag" which you fill and send back for free, then receive either cash or store credit for the items the company wants to resell. You can choose to have the unwanted clothes either go to charity or come back to you.
- **Motherhoodcloset.com.** Mail your used, but "clean, stylish maternity clothes" to this online consignment store, and you'll receive cash for those items that sell within 120 days.
- **Replacements.com.** This is a well-regarded site on which to sell china, stoneware, glassware, silver, stainless, and collectibles.

Assessing Your House's Best Features

Now that you've gotten thoroughly depressed about your house's little (or big) dings in need of repair, start creating a list of your home's positive features. Some of the items that we suggest may require a little research.

This isn't just for the sake of your mood, of course. Even the most knowledgeable agent may not pick up on all the great features of your home or neighborhood, which means you can ultimately contribute to the success of marketing your home by collecting and conveying this information.

What's More Important: Number of Bedrooms and Bathrooms or Square Footage?

Read the real estate ads, and you'll notice that the number of bedrooms and bathrooms in a house always gets announced front and center— while square footage gets little attention. Yet a tiny house might have more bedrooms and bathrooms stuffed into it than a luxury abode.

The reason, as you might guess, is that one of the first considerations on homebuyers' minds is how many children and others can share the home, and possibly how many rooms they can use as private offices or work spaces. Most buyers would like a home with at least three bedrooms. So, an additional bedroom and bathroom can instantly bump a home's value up by tens of thousands of dollars.

That's not to say that square footage is irrelevant. When it comes time for a home to be professionally appraised, the appraiser will certainly take it into account. Part of the reason an additional room raises the value is that the house itself is probably larger. If it's not, perhaps having sacrificed space in the kitchen or living room to a bedroom, the appraised value may go down again. In fact, lawsuits have been brought by buyers angry about discovering that the home's square footage was not as much as originally advertised.

The lesson here is to know your house's square footage, and double-check it before advertising if you suspect that past measurements (in tax records and otherwise) might be wrong. If you have few bedrooms and bathrooms but lots of square footage, be sure to advertise the home's spacious feel. But don't get frustrated if, for lack of bedrooms and bathrooms, some buyers simply aren't interested.

TIP

What's your house's "Walk Score?" The closer your house is to restaurants, shops, schools, and other amenities, the higher it will rate on this scale, found at www.walkscore.com. If you rank high, be sure to advertise it! The website (and app) also let you calculate the time it takes to get around by walking, biking, or using mass transit.

Here are some features (beyond the usual "bed, bath, and basement") that will be of particular interest to buyers (or in some cases, to subsets of buyers):

- an intriguing back story (did a famous person live there, or did a known architect design it?)
- excellent school district (this raises your home's value instantly—have you looked at private school tuition lately?)
- easy commute to nearest city or work hub
- desirable neighborhood, with shops, restaurants, parks, and so on
- eat-in kitchen, or a kitchen island (buyers love, love, love high-end kitchens)
- en-suite master bath, and preferably two sinks
- space for a home office
- recent remodeling or upgrades
- high-end appliances
- hardwood floors
- fireplace (get the chimney sweep in to make sure it works!)
- large, walk-in closets (the desirability of which you can observe on most any HGTV show)
- up-to-date technological features, including automation and smart-home capabilities
- built within last five years
- urban amenities (most likely found in a condo or townhome), such as a round-the-clock concierge, a gym, and a pool/spa
- minimal maintenance, if it's a condo, townhome, or other property within a planned community
- in an older home, interesting historic features, and
- low crime rate locally.

Your home might also have unique features worth noting. For example, let's say you had an architect draw up plans to convert your garage into living space, but decided to move before starting the project. You might leave the plans—and reassurance that the city had responded favorably about the prospects of permit approval—for prospective buyers to look at and eventually keep.

> **TIP**
> **Save clippings about your city or neighborhood.** Any positive press—a great review of a local restaurant, a write-up in a travel magazine, or an award such as "Most Exciting City of 20xx"—can help your home stand out to prospective buyers. Setting out a packet of these at an open house is a fine strategy (and don't forget to provide URLs in case people want to look these up themselves).

Aiming for a Particular Sale Date?

Assuming that your informal evaluation of your house's condition didn't turn up huge repair needs, and that you want to sell it in the relatively near future, the next question is whether you should aim for an actual sale date. Kicking things into high gear can be stressful, for obvious reasons—but may be worth it. Factors to consider include:

- **Are outside circumstances pushing you to sell quickly?** If, for instance, you've already bought another home or invested in a retirement community and need to cash out of this home to pay for the next, then the obvious answer is yes, you need to sell ASAP. You could have your home on the market in a matter of days—but it's not the ideal scenario.
- **When's the best selling season in your area?** Real estate markets tend to be weakest in cold, dreary winter months (who wants to look at houses in the rain or snow?) and strongest in the spring, when the sun is shining and flowers are blooming. Of course, if you live in an area with year-round sun, such seasonal considerations are reduced. And putting your house

on the market during a slow season does mean you won't have much competition. But you'll still be affected by the fact that parents who need to put their children into a new school prefer to move during the summer, to avoid shifts between school districts. And due to holidays and vacations, December tends to be the absolute worst month to put a house on the market, followed closely by August. If you're thinking, "Why not just put the house on the market during a slow period and keep it there?" realize that others have tried that strategy and regretted it. A house that remains unsold for several months starts to appear "stale," with buyers wondering what's wrong with it. You may end up having to lower your price.

*L*esson learned the hard way — **We should have waited until springtime.** "Putting our house on the market right before Thanksgiving turned out to be a big mistake," says Kathleen. "Only two offers came in and both were so far under our asking price that we didn't even bother to counteroffer. We considered lowering the list price, but fortunately had some flexibility on our move date. So we decided to take the house off the market and relist it in the spring. The mood among buyers was completely different then! We soon received five solid offers, and sold without further hitches."

- **Is your local real estate market on the upswing?** If prices are rising rapidly in your area, you might earn more by waiting. Then again, if you'll be looking to buy your next home, it too will be rising in value while you wait—and beating out the competition may be stressful when the market is that much hotter. (See Chapter 6 for more on analyzing where your local market is going.)
- **Is there some reason to wait longer before selling?** For instance, if you've owned and lived in the house for a little under two years, and it has appreciated in value such that you might owe capital gains taxes, you might want to make sure the sale happens after a full two years has passed—which is the only way you'll qualify for a capital gains tax exclusion of $250,000

for individuals or $500,000 for married couples filing jointly. (See the "Selling a House" section in Nolo.com's Real Estate Area for articles on the capital gains tax.)

Your real estate agent can help you settle on the best date to list your home. An accountant's advice may also be helpful for tax questions.

What Else Is for Sale in Your Area?

Here's another task you can start on as soon as you're ready—and it's a fun one. You'll want to get a sense of the local market, so that you can see where your house fits in and be alert to any market changes as they occur.

Start by reading the local real estate listings. Notice what features the ads highlight (meaning what the real estate agents who wrote them think will best attract buyers). Later, you can consider whether your house has those features, or whether they might be added without major effort or expense. (More on making those decisions in Chapter 3.)

You'll also, of course, want to pay attention to the list price of houses that appear comparable to yours—bearing in mind that the list price won't necessarily match the eventual sale price. In a hot market, prices may be set artificially low, on the assumption that they will be bid up, perhaps even beyond their "real" value. In a cold market, prices may come down after negotiations with buyers who know they've got leverage.

Next, begin visiting open houses in your neighborhood and surrounding ones. No need to be stealthy about this: Real estate agents are accustomed to home visitors who aren't serious buyers. In fact, they see you as a potential customer, and may be all-too eager to offer you their services. (Don't sign up anyone before going through all the steps described in Chapter 2.)

As you visit homes, put yourself in the shoes of a prospective homebuyer, paying attention to what attracts you, as well as to what other visitors "ooh" and "ahh" over. Be sure to pick up any listing sheets and promotional materials, and study the home's features. If you feel a certain shock when reading that a home needs "$20,000 pest repair," make a mental note that your buyers may, someday, feel a similar shock.

If a home you're looking at has been "staged," consider what you like and don't like about the result, and whether you'd use that stager yourself.

All of this advance work will make you much better able to come to an agreement with your real estate agent about how to market your home and what price is appropriate (covered in Chapter 6). There's nothing worse for a home's marketability than when, for example, the real estate agent whispers to buyers at the open house that he or she tried to talk the seller into a lower price, but the seller just wasn't being realistic. It happens.

Let's Play, Guess the List Price!

After you've spent some time visiting open houses and getting to know your local market, you might test your newfound knowledge. Make a game out of walking through the open house *before* peeking at the list price. Then guess what that figure is.

When your guesses get within about $20,000 to $50,000 of the actual list price (if it's a home within the median range), you're almost ready to figure out what your own house is worth—or at least, should realistically be listed at.

How Much Will You Spend to Sell Your Home?

Wait, isn't this supposed to be about bringing in a big check when you sell? Yes, but let's not forget that, for maximum return, you'll need to invest some cash up front. Fortunately, by planning ahead, you may find ways to reduce some of the costs, perhaps by handling tasks yourself or getting competing bids for work. Here's a rundown of what expenses to expect.

Painting. A new paint job, inside and out, is one of most cost-effective ways to freshen up a house in advance of a sale. If you've recently painted, this is less important—though if your color choices were bold or unique, you might want to tone them down with some crowd-pleasing neutrals. Your real estate agent or stager, if you hire one (see Chapter 5) can advise you about the best colors. Home painting typically costs several thousand dollars, at a minimum.

Window washing. When did you last wash your windows—especially on the outside panes of upper floors? Sparkling windows make a surprisingly big difference to buyer perceptions. Hiring someone will cost a few hundred dollars, depending on the size and height of your home.

Carpet deep cleaning. Dirt and dust tend to accumulate in carpets, creating a vast swath of surface area that looks less than fresh. Angie's List members say that they paid around $45 per room in 2013.

Fixups. Which repairs are necessary (such as replacing cracked windows or stained carpeting) and which (such as major remodels) should be left for the buyer to take on is, again, separately discussed in Chapter 3. But there's practically no house that couldn't use at least a few hundred dollars' worth of quick maintenance to make sure it looks well-cared for and leaves fewer items for a home inspector to comment on.

Staging. It's de rigeur in some parts of the United States, and less known in others—but staging your home, or having a decorator help declutter, reorganize, and in some cases refurnish it after you've moved your stuff out, can give it a whole new look. Studies show that buyers pay more for staged homes. Expect to pay a professional stager a few thousand dollars for these services (a bit less if some of your own furniture is usable.)

Adding decorative or new items to your home (if you're not hiring a stager). You're almost guaranteed to have to buy things like a new doormat, new plush towels for the bathroom, flowers for the showings, and more, depending on what your house already has.

Other likely possibilities include new couch cushions, area rugs, a nice table runner, and artwork to replace your wall of kids' photos.

Landscaping. Buyers are increasingly interested in the state of your garden. If it's already fully planted, you'll want to hire someone (or put in some sweat equity) to get it raked, pruned, and otherwise tidied up. If the area hasn't already been landscaped, plan to add some new greenery and flowering plants. (By the way, if you plant in containers, you can take these with you when you move—unless they're so big or incorporated into the property as to be considered "fixtures.") Many sellers simply put in new sod (grass). (But if you go this route, at least do the buyers a favor and don't leave the plastic mesh backing on it, in case the buyers want to replace it with something more interesting and environmentally friendly—especially in drought-ridden parts of the country. That plastic stuff is hard to dig out.)

Preinspection reports. Having a professional inspect your house for either termite/pest damage or other structural matters isn't required, nor expected in most parts of the United States. Buyers expect to pay for their own inspectors, and in fact will probably want to hire ones they know and trust regardless of whether you've had the property inspected first. Yet, as we'll discuss in Chapter 3, you might want to have the house inspected before letting buyers in. This could be a good strategy if, for example, you've owned the property for many years and wonder whether any problems have arisen that you're oblivious to, and would perhaps prefer to fix before buyers have a chance to get upset about them. Inspections will run you upwards of $200.

Lights and heat while the house sits empty. If you'll be moving out before putting your house on the market, expect to pay double utilities for a while. You'll want to leave the lights and heat on in the house, or program them to stay on during any hours that potential buyers and their agents may be stopping by the place. No one likes to enter a cold, dark house and fumble around for the light switches. To estimate how much this will be, check your regular monthly bills, subtracting a little to account for the fact that you won't be living there.

Extra homeowners' insurance for the vacancy period. Check with your homeowners' insurance carrier. Your insurance may not apply when the home is "vacant," which term will be defined in your policy. You can ask for a rider to cover any period of vacancy or buy a separate, short-term policy.

> **TIP**
>
> **Save those receipts!** If you might owe capital gains tax on your profits (unlikely unless the home appreciated greatly in value while you lived there), some of your prep work might qualify as home "improvements," which will reduce your taxable gains. (Unfortunately, basic repairs and other physical changes to the property to make it look good to buyers do not offer any tax benefits.) See an accountant for a full analysis.

At the closing (described in Chapter 10) and after, you will face some additional expenses. The good news is, most of what you'll be paying out at the closing will come out of your sale proceeds. The bad news is, you'll be saying goodbye to some big dollars.

Real estate agent commissions. You, as the seller, will likely be paying the entire 5% – 6% commission, to be split between the buyer's agent and yours. For ways to reduce this figure, see Chapter 2.

Other closing costs or credits to the buyer. You might have agreed—based on local tradition or buyer negotiation—to pay some of the standard costs associated with closing the deal, such as fees for the escrow company; the mortgage and home appraisal; recording and transfer of the property; homeowners' and title insurance; and more. When the market is down, buyers have been known to ask sellers to pay all of the closing costs, which typically add up to 2% to 4% of the selling price.

Transfer taxes. Your city or state may require you to pay transfer taxes, as a percentage of the sale price. In some localities, these can be surprisingly high.

Home warranty for the buyer. Whether because the buyer requests it or to make the buyer feel secure about the home purchase, many sellers purchase a home warranty on the buyer's behalf. This is a service contract that covers repairs to appliances and certain systems within the house for the first year of ownership. It will cost between about $300 and $900, depending in part on the house itself and on where you live.

Capital gains tax. If you earn less than $250,000 on your home sale (or $500,000 if you're married and filing jointly), you aren't likely to owe a thing in the way of capital gains taxes. But if you earn more than that, or don't meet the other qualifications for the exclusion (the house was your principal residence, and you lived there for two out of the five years before selling it or qualify for an exception) you'll want to look further into the matter. Once you've subtracted things like the costs of preparing the property for sale from the supposed gains, you may not owe any tax after all.

Moving costs. Getting help from your friends with pickup trucks will save you some dough—but will take a lot more time. Sometimes it's worth paying for the deluxe treatment, where the company packs your boxes for you, transports them to the new location, and unpacks at the other end. But it comes at a price— typically upwards of $10,000. The more you do yourself, the less you'll pay Various moving cost calculators can be found online, such as at www.moving.com.

Homeowners' association fees. If you're in a community governed by a homeowners' association (HOA), you may need to pay for various items, starting with a certificate of compliance showing that the condition of your property isn't violating any HOA rules and you are up to date on your fees and assessments. You will likely also need to pay a fee for copies of all the documents (Covenants, Conditions, & Restrictions or "CC & Rs" and so forth) that you must provide to your prospective buyer. Check with your HOA for the details— but expect to pay several hundred dollars at least. Do this sooner rather than later—some HOAs move slowly on such requests, and you'll pay more if you have to ask for a rush. What's more, you may have to make repairs or other changes to bring your property into compliance. For example, your HOA may require that you replace a dead tree on your property before you close on your home. ●

Getting Expert Help: Hiring a Real Estate Agent, Lawyer, and Accountant

U nless you're already a real estate pro (in which case you probably wouldn't be reading this book), you'll probably want to sign up an agent to list and help sell your property. Then add a lawyer to the mix, if you either live in one of the U.S. states where legal help with a real estate transaction is required or if your transaction is particularly complex. An accountant's advice may also be useful for tax and related issues. We'll discuss when, why, and how to hire one or all of these pros in this chapter.

Hiring a Real Estate Agent

They go by various names: real estate agent, real estate broker, or in the case of someone who's a member of the National Association of Realtors® (NAR), Realtor®. All of these folks are qualified to do the same basic thing: help people list, market, and sell their home. A good agent is a combination salesperson, marketing guru, organizer, negotiator, creative thinker, problem solver, and just plain hard worker.

Of course, you don't get all that for free. In fact, one of your biggest expenses in selling your home will be paying the agent. The standard payment method is by commission, typically 5% to 6% of the home's selling price.

Your agent doesn't pocket the full amount: It's usually split in half with the buyer's agent, after which your agent divvies up what's left with the listing agency or broker (the agent's boss). Also, your agent bears many of the costs of marketing your property, which can be significant.

The standard commission model has plenty of critics. You might soon become one of them, particularly if your home is at the luxury end of the spectrum or you live in an area with sky-high real estate prices for homes of any size. Why should you have to pay a real estate broker $40,000 to sell your $800,000 home when, if you lived in a smaller place worth $400,000, the commission would be a mere (though hardly insignificant) $20,000? Will the agent really provide $20,000 more in services for the larger place? Probably not.

Indeed, a few variations of the standard commission model have been tried—and many have failed. Discount brokers typically offer lower commissions in return for customers performing more tasks on their own, but they've often found either that customers want more handholding or that they're shunned by traditional brokers. The upshot is that if you sell your house via a discount broker, you might find that buyers' agents discourage their clients from visiting your property.

One company trying a hybrid model that may hold promise is Redfin, which charges sellers a 4.5% commission—the buyer's agent gets the standard 3%, but the Redfin agent gets only a 1.5% commission. The company provides additional compensation to its agents through salaries and bonuses based on customer satisfaction.

With all that in mind, we're going to assume that you'll be paying your agent a sizable commission. In that case, you want to hire an agent whose high-quality work will justify that payment. In this chapter, we'll explain:

- reasons to hire an agent
- how to choose an agent, and
- ways to negotiate the agent's commission.

SKIP AHEAD

Can you save money by selling without an agent? It's possible, but not always practical. Chapter 11 will discuss the pros and cons of selling "FSBO" (for sale by owner).

How a Good Agent Adds Value

Experienced agents do a lot to earn their commission. Their knowledge, market savvy, and effort will save you time and energy. Ultimately, it may get your house sold quickly and for more money than you could have earned on your own. That's probably why 89% of home sellers use an agent's services (according to 2013 figures from the National Association of Realtors).

The main tasks your agent will handle include:

- **Recommending an appropriate price.** As Chapter 6 will cover, setting the right price is a must from the get-go. If you overprice, you risk having your house sitting unsold for weeks or even months, until no one wants to look at it anymore. If you underprice, you could lose money, particularly if the house doesn't inspire multiple bids. With access to important market information, agents will know how to hit the right balance, and suggest a range for you to choose within.

- **Helping you prepare the house for sale.** True, your real estate agent won't ordinarily clean or pack up your boxes of clutter, nor force you to do so. (Though, says agent Amy Robeson, "I once had a client who was a bit of a hoarder; I visited her at home every day for a while, to cheer her on as she went through her stuff.") A good agent will have enough experience to offer highly specific information and advice about what needs doing (or not) and how to make the house look its best, having prepared many homes for sale in the past.

- **Recommending repair people, cleaners, painters, gardeners, movers, auction houses, and so on.** A good agent knows who to call for the various tasks that need doing in order to make your house show well and to help you at every phase of the sales process. The agent can give you names, and may even help contact or coordinate these service providers. But don't expect the agent to foot the bill (an all-too-common misunderstanding by home sellers).

- **Advertising the property for sale.** A major factor in getting your house sold is making sure that as many buyers as possible know it's on the market. An experienced agent will draw on an existing network of personal connections and company resources to make this happen—and will, for the most part, pay the marketing bills. (But don't expect the agent to lay out cash for repairs and improvements in the name of "marketing.") The agent may commission drawings and photographs of your house, write ad copy, create listing sheets or brochures, and advertise the house by posting it on the MLS and other online listing portals, create a unique website, carry out email or snail mail campaigns, talk up the place to fellow brokers, hold open houses (both for other agents and for the public), and more. For a more detailed discussion of marketing strategies, see Chapter 7.

Best thing we ever did **Choose a Realtor who was active in local real estate networks.** Says Linda, "I'd been in touch with my Realtor about selling (he'd also helped me buy that same house), but hadn't gotten around to signing the listing agreement yet. At a Realtors' get-together, he spoke of my house to a colleague. She thought she might have an interested buyer from out of town. They came to my house on a Sunday morning just before her departure. The result was that I sold my house for the asking price to the first person who saw it, before it was ever listed."

- **Handling inquiries from prospective buyers.** When interested buyers want to look at your house or get more information, they'll call your agent, not you. This can be a big plus if someone ignores the "Do Not Disturb Occupants" sign that may be attached to your "For Sale" sign and knocks on your door. You have no obligation to engage with people in this situation (especially the rude ones who ignore a sign) and can politely advise them how to reach your agent.
- **Showing the property to prospective purchasers.** Your real estate agent may walk prospective buyers through your home privately as well as at open houses. A surprising number of buyers call the selling agent directly after seeing a home listed online or getting the agent's number from the "For Sale" sign. They may not have hired their own agent, or their agent may be away when they want to visit the home. The expectation is that the listing agent will be available on short notice for such showings. (If an unrepresented buyer is seriously interested in the place, the question arises whether your agent can and should represent both of you simultaneously, as discussed in "Avoid Dual Agency," below.)

- **Ensuring buyers receive proper disclosures.** Chances are, your state's laws require you to disclose certain known problems with your home to prospective purchasers, by filling out a standard form. Additionally, you may be required to make certain environmental disclosures—for example, if your house is old enough, a disclosure that it may contain lead-based paint. And your city may add other requirements to the mix— perhaps that you disclose whether any deaths have occurred on the property. Your agent will explain what information you must provide, will probably give you a standard form or set of forms that meet the legal requirements, and may also need to fill out a portion of the forms him- or herself.

> (!) CAUTION
> **Your agent's job does not include helping hide the house's problems.** As described by California Realtor Carol Neil, "I know there are times when home sellers wish their agents would just keep certain bits of information under their bonnet! However, any agent that you'd want to hire will be careful to ensure that the disclosures are fully made, telling everything the seller knows."

- **Hearing offers.** When someone—or better yet, a bunch of someones—offer to purchase your home, your agent will be the one to receive these offers on your behalf. Although the offers themselves will likely be in writing, buyers' agents often ask to meet with the listing agent in person, to "present" the offer. This basically means the buyers' agents take about five to ten minutes to make a pitch summarizing the offer terms and explaining why you should choose to sell to this "wonderful young couple" or whoever the agent represents. You may attend these presentations, but your agent will be largely running the show.
- **Reviewing offers and negotiating a deal.** After the offers are in and the buyers' agents have left, the agent will review the offers with you, explain any confusing spots, give you advice

on the strengths and weaknesses of each offer, suggest what to ask for or concede in any counteroffers, and explain any areas of concern. The agent can help evaluate whether the highest-priced offer is truly the best one, and decide which one to accept. Then, the agent will work with the buyer's agent to iron out the terms of the deal (perhaps with assistance from your attorneys), protecting your interests in the process.

- **Making sure everything gets wrapped up by the closing date.** Once you and the buyer have reached an agreement, you'll have to make sure all the steps leading up to the closing (during what's called the escrow period) are properly completed. An important part of this will be making sure that all contract contingencies are met and released by the dates stated in the agreement. That may involve, for example, making your house available for inspections, and following up by arranging for repairs. Your agent (and possibly also your attorney) will work with you, the buyer's agent, and the title or escrow officer to coordinate all of this. An important part of the process is negotiating over repair costs after the inspection, a time when many deals fall through because the buyer either asks for an unreasonable amount or the buyer and seller get angry and refuse to compromise.

The above is simply an outline of what the typical agent must do in a normal transaction. Every home sale is unique, however. An intrepid agent may end up taking on a variety of tasks when there's no one else to handle them: from sweeping the front porch to researching where to get an unusual bit of carpentry done to arranging for a string quartet to play at a gala open house for a luxury home. Agent Amy Robeson says, "I had one client whose husband had already moved to start his new job in another country, and she needed to pack up her children and sell the house in order to join him. I told her to just leave behind whatever she couldn't pack up and I'd take care of it. I also made sure the lawn got mowed before the new owner moved in." (Don't expect all of these things out of your agent, however!)

Finding and Choosing a Top-Notch Agent

You've probably heard or read that the real estate market is flooded with agents. Critics of the burgeoning industry have some valid concerns: Getting a real estate license is easier to accomplish than in some other professions, which means there are many unskilled agents out there. And some agents enter the market only part time, making it difficult for their customers to work with and rely on them.

The good news is that, after the recent slowdown in U.S. real estate, scores of less-serious and less-qualified agents packed up and left the profession. Still, not every remaining agent is someone with whom you'd want to work. You'll need to invest some time in finding the best.

Lesson learned the hard way **Hiring my friend as our agent wasn't the smartest idea.** Explains Sarabel, "We've been friends for a long time, and I respect the fact that she's learning the ropes from her mother, who's an experienced Realtor. Still, every time anything to do with numbers comes up, she says, 'Let's ask my mother.' Sometimes we have meetings with her mother alone. This isn't inspiring confidence that she's ready for this transaction, and I worry that there's no one who's entirely focused on it."

Reasons to Choose Carefully

Remember, you pay the same commission percentage to an agent whether you get horrible service or wonderful service. While one agent may be willing to spend long hours aggressively marketing your house or helping you pack up stuff for Goodwill, another may stifle a yawn as he or she posts its description on the local MLS website and lets it sit. (It's small comfort that, if the house ends up selling for less than it could have, the agent will earn less.)

Now, are you ready for a surprising statistic? Two-thirds of home sellers in 2013 contacted only one agent before signing that person up to list their home. Is the world full of careless home sellers? Perhaps not: Approximately the same number of sellers either used the same agent they'd worked with previously in buying or selling a home, or got a referral from a friend or family member. So they already knew of someone they could trust, as perhaps you do, too (in which case you can skip ahead to the portion of this chapter that deals with signing the listing agreement).

Agent? Broker? What's the Difference?

Technically speaking, what you're looking for is a real estate salesperson. That person may have either a salesperson's license or a broker's license. At a minimum, a salesperson's license is needed to represent someone in a real estate transaction, while a broker's license means the individual has undergone additional training and may act in a managerial capacity over other agents. When you sign a listing agreement with your agent, you'll probably need the approval of the managing broker in the real estate office. (Many real estate agents have a broker's license but don't act as managing brokers, however.)

You might never meet the managing broker at your agent's company. However, if you have problems with your agent, or if your transaction is particularly complicated, the managing broker may get involved. He or she will also take a cut of the commission you pay—most likely, half of what your agent gets.

But if you don't already have an agent you'd like to work with—or you wonder whether you should really hire the agent that your friend recommends even though he's never worked with the agent and the agent is his ex-brother-in-law and behind on child-support payments—you definitely want to speak with more than one agent before making your choice.

Later in this chapter, we'll give you a list of specific questions you can ask prospective agents. You're looking for an agent with experience (at least a few years as a residential real estate agent) and education (such as professional courses and certifications). But you should seek out other characteristics as well: someone who is detail-oriented, trustworthy, personable (you'll be working together a lot, plus counting on the agent to get along well with buyers), flexible, and able to adapt to challenging market conditions. Above all else, you're looking for results: an agent with a proven track record of getting homes sold.

Getting Recommendations for Excellent Listing Agents

Start by asking friends, colleagues, and neighbors for the names of agents they've worked with to sell their homes. Neighbors are a particularly good bet, since any agents they've worked with likely know the area well. Some may be able to offer only the names of people they *don't* recommend, but that can be helpful too—you can narrow down your list, especially if you get more than one negative report on the same agent.

If you liked the agent who helped you buy the home but he or she works only with buyers, ask that agent for recommendations of respectable listing agents. Alternatively, if you were impressed with the listing agent for the seller who sold the house to you, that may be the logical place to start.

You might also contact local professionals in related fields, such as your accountant or attorney. They've probably worked with real estate professionals and may have good recommendations.

Checking Out Agents Online

The availability of online reviews and ratings of real estate agents is slowly catching up to that of, say, restaurants. You may want to cross-check a variety of sites, such as Yelp, Zillow, Trulia, and NeighborCity.

Some state Realtor associations also collect customer reviews, and agents may post client reviews on their own websites. (Yes, these are preselected, but you can always ask to personally speak to references. Besides, the agent's website is also a great place to learn about the agent's personality, credentials, and professionalism.) Redfin routinely posts customer reviews, since its business model depends on rewarding agents with proven records of customer satisfaction.

Showing a Prospective Agent Your Home

Eventually, you'll narrow your list to a few agents and then ask each one a set of detailed questions to help you select the right one to sell your home. But first, the prospective agents will want to *see* that home.

At your initial meeting, the agent will most likely come to your house and take a look around. The agent will use the information gleaned from that visit to create what's called a comparable market analysis (CMA). (When prepared by a broker, it may be called a "broker's price opinion," or BPO.)

The CMA (or BPO) identifies recently sold homes in your area that were most like yours, and tells you at what price they sold. The agents will want to look at your home's specific features, so as to best compare them with the other homes. No two houses are exactly alike, and upgrades or special features your house has that comparable properties don't can raise its value (or vice versa).

Best thing we ever did — **Watched agents' reactions as they toured my home.** According to Gracie, "I met with three agents before choosing one, and each spent over an hour looking through the place and talking to us. That let me get a sense of their personalities, too. There was one who, though he seemed knowledgeable and hardworking, just didn't seem enthusiastic about the place. (We had remodeled extensively, and it had an unusual modern design.) The agent we chose seemed to 'get' the house, and to love it as we had. She ended up being great to work with—we're still friends!"

Evaluating the Agent's Presentation

If you like what you've seen of a particular agent so far, it's time to arrange another meeting. At that meeting the agent will provide you with the full, written CMA that he or she has compiled in the meantime. You should also ask any of the questions on the below interview list that weren't covered in your first meeting.

The CMA should include all properties sold in the last three to six months that are truly comparable to yours—that is, are similar in size, location, amenities, and so forth. The report should also reflect any credits that the sellers of those properties gave the buyers for repairs—in other words, IOUs to be paid from the proceeds of the sale—which essentially function as reductions to the selling price. (Such information isn't public—they'll have gotten it from the "agents-only" section of the MLS.) And, the CMA should include comps currently on the market or awaiting offers, to give you a complete picture of the very latest price trends.

> **TIP**
>
> **Make sure the agent (or someone within his or her office) has actually visited most of the houses listed on your CMA.** If not, the agent doesn't know much more than you do about each property: its location and size, when it was listed and for how much, and when and if it sold and for how much. But an agent's personal knowledge of those other properties— for example, that a house had an awkward floor plan or that its master bathroom was recently remodeled—will be fundamental in determining how comparable they really are.

You'll also want to get information about the agent's sales history. Ask for a transaction report for the last year. This should contain the address, size, and number of rooms for each house the agent listed; the listing and sales dates; and the listing and sales prices and ratio. The object is to find out whether the agent sells homes regularly in your area; how long it takes the agent to sell properties, on average (the "DOM" or "days on market" figure); whether there are any "dead spots" in the agent's history (if so, you can inquire as to why); whether the agent's listings are receiving multiple offers; and whether the agent sets realistic list prices, which bring in sales at above, not below, the list price. Though there's no way to get the entire picture just from the numbers, they give you a great starting point for asking more questions and for comparing agents.

Avoid Dual Agency

As a home seller, you want your agent to represent your interests and help you achieve your goal: to sell your home quickly, for as much money as possible. On the other side of the table is the buyer, who's hoping for the opposite: to get the property for as little as possible. So if a buyer shows up unrepresented, should your agent agree to handle the entire transaction for both of you, as a "dual agent"?

Dual agency was once traditional in the real estate industry. But things have shifted, so that most sellers and buyers expect to have their own agents by their sides. Nevertheless, some sellers think they'll save money by using a dual agent (who might then offer a lower commission).

But experience has shown that it's difficult for one agent to represent *both* buyer and seller. As Massachusetts Realtor Nancy Atwood explains, "The listing agent has a fiduciary duty to represent the interests of the seller—to get the seller the best deal possible. A dual agent then has the same duty to the buyer. These are opposite goals, the result being that the agent ends up really being nobody's agent, because it's impossible to represent both interests fully."

If you're going to pay a full commission, you want someone who fully represents your interests. If an agent asks you to consent to a dual agency—such consent being typically required by law—we recommend denying the request. Even better, ask any agent you're considering hiring, "Would you ever represent me in a dual agency?" That gets the issue out of the way early on.

Somewhat less onerous than dual agency is what's called "designated agency." Here, the buyer is represented by another agent in the same brokerage as your agent. Technically, this is a form of dual agency, because each agent works for the same broker. Unlike a dual agency, you get personal representation from a designated agent. But you must fully trust your agent to represent your interests and not divulge your bottom line to the buyer's agent.

If you're willing to participate in a designated agency, you might request a reduction in the commission based on the fact that the brokerage will make twice as much as it otherwise would have on the deal.

CAUTION
Make sure your prospective agent's experience isn't limited to representing buyers. Berkeley Realtor Daniel Stea explains, "New or young realtors tend to start by representing buyers, because it's easier. If a buyers' agent is good and committed, and invests in marketing his or her services, the agent will start getting sellers as clients. A Realtor with a lot of listings probably had a lot of buyers over the years to get there. They're rising to the top." So, do you want to be among the first to hire an agent who hasn't handled the selling end of the transaction before? Maybe not—or at least not without assurances that the agent has the backing of a top-quality agency and will be getting good advice from colleagues—which is a good reason to ask questions about this.

The other thing the agent should present is a marketing plan for your home. This will be part background information—you'll probably learn about the agent's experience and history—but should be mostly focused on the agent's strategy for bringing your home to the attention of interested buyers. If it seems like the agent is going to repeat a "tried and true" marketing plan, and the agent's sales numbers don't look exceptional, you can expect the same treatment everyone else gets, with the same potentially mediocre results.

"I spend a lot of time doing a 'premarketing plan,'" says Realtor Mark Nash. "For example, I frequently get clients who are moving their elderly parents into care facilities and are selling the family home, which may need painting, updating, new landscaping, and so forth. I give them a list of things to do, and only after they've done them do we go in and take pictures and draw up marketing material that can highlight the positive changes."

CAUTION
Don't settle for a phone interview. A prospective agent may promise to compile an adequate CMA just by talking to you on the phone. If so, it's a red flag: The agent isn't willing to put in the time to really understand how much your house is worth and how to position it competitively. Cross that agent off your list.

After doing the CMA, the agent should be able to suggest a prospective list price, or a range within which the listing price should fall, subject to changes in the market between your meeting date and when the listing goes live. The range should be fairly small: Hitting within the closest $50,000 or $100,000 hardly takes an expert.

Some agents, but by no means all, use their estimated list price as an opportunity to "reel you in," by giving you an unrealistically high figure. This is called "buying" the listing, and assumes you'll believe that the agent in question has the magic touch to sell your house for that amount. If the list price is too high, however, it could easily have the opposite effect—your house will sit on the market, perhaps without attracting any interested buyers. Make sure the agent is providing you with solid, recent data to back up any suggested list price.

Also ask whether the agent has a particular pricing philosophy. Some, for example, may have found that in your area, starting with the lowest rational price is the most effective way to bring in good offers.

Checklist: Items to Ask Agents For

At your meeting, the prospective agent should give you:

☐ the agent's CMA for your home

☐ information about the agent's sales history in the last year, and

☐ a comprehensive marketing plan/presentation.

Final Questions to Ask a Prospective Agent

In addition to getting the information discussed above, your meetings with prospective agents provide an opportunity to ask questions. You're the boss here: You're looking for an agent who can really demonstrate an ability to get things done. Spend as long as you need to get all these and any other questions answered:

- **How long have you been a real estate agent?** It's best to work with someone who has at least three years' experience in the residential real estate market where you live—even more is preferable.
- **Are you a Realtor?** Membership in the National Association of Realtors (NAR) shows a continued interest in professional development, as well as a basic commitment to ethical behavior.
- **Do you have a broker's license?** To sell real estate, an agent needs only a salesperson's license. A broker's license is an extra step—again, evidence of the agent's commitment to professional development.
- **Do you have any professional designations or have you taken any specialized courses?** The NAR offers special designations for real estate agents, such as Certified Residential Specialist® (CRS®). Additionally, agents can take many different training classes to gain additional knowledge.
- **Will you be providing me with a comparable market analysis?** If you haven't already received the CMA, the answer should be a definite "yes." You want actual data to help price your home accurately.
- **Are you available on a full-time basis?** It's imperative that your agent be readily available to respond to inquiries and show the property. While agents can't work around the clock, many routinely put in time on nights and weekends. Eliminate any agent who doesn't work full time or doesn't have a backup plan that you're completely comfortable with, for example coverage by a fellow agent in the same office.
- **Would you ever represent me as a dual agent?** As already explained, you want an agent who represents your interests alone.
- **How many residential real estate transactions have you been a part of in the last year?** This should be a minimum of ten, to show that the agent is actively practicing.
- **In how many transactions did you represent the seller?** You want this to be at least half. Also ask how many of the houses sold.
- **Do you specialize in a certain type of property?** If so, make sure it's the kind of property you're selling: for example, a condominium, or an older home in a historic neighborhood.

- **Do you specialize in a certain geographic area?** Again, you'll want to make sure that if an agent has this type of specialty, it's in the area where you live. (Keep in mind that if you're buying in another area nearby and plan to use the same agent for both transactions, the agent probably won't be as experienced in the area where you're looking to buy.)

- **How will I reach you?** Are there days or times the agent is unavailable or will be on vacation? You want to know that it will be easy for you to call and check in and that the agent hasn't planned any lengthy hiatuses. Also make sure you're going to get personal service—that is, you're not going to be pushed off onto an aide.

- **How would you prepare my home for sale?** This is where the agent will describe any experience with staging and prepping a house for sale. While the agent may not want to give away "tricks of the trade" until you have a listing agreement, you're justified in asking for a general idea of what needs to be done, as well as for photos and ideas that explain what the agent has done to help other sellers.

- **What was the difference between the list price and selling price of homes you sold in the last year?** This is more of the hard data you'll need in evaluating whether the agent is realistic when pricing homes. If an agent tells you, "You can put your house on the market for $600,000," but similar listings by the agent at that price sold for only $550,000, you'll have a better idea of what you're in for.

- **How long did the houses you've sold in the last six months take to sell?** If the agent's listings are languishing on the market for weeks or months, that's what you can expect, too—perhaps because your home won't be priced appropriately, or because the agent doesn't do enough to promote the sale. However, an agent may also have good explanations for aberrations on past listings—for example, an unreasonable seller who insisted on listing a property above market value or a house that needed major repairs and was therefore unappealing to most buyers.

- **How many buyers and sellers are you currently representing?** Don't sign up with someone who's too busy to spend significant amounts of time with you. If the number sounds suspiciously high (say, above ten or so total clients at any given time) find out how the agent gets things done.

CAUTION

There's no "right" number of clients. As Realtor Nancy Atwood explains, "Different agents can handle varying levels of work. While one agent may have her hands full with five clients, another may be able to take on ten and still provide excellent service." Use the agent's response to this question to find out how much time the agent spends taking care of each property and how available the agent will be to help sell yours.

- **How exactly would you market my property—and how is this superior to what other agents might do?** Give the agent the opportunity to present you with a comprehensive marketing plan and to sell you on his or her services. You want to know that you're going to approach the process systematically, and that the agent has an attractive website and other resources and ideas for marketing your house effectively.
- **Would you provide references?** Ask for at least three names of current or former clients who sold their homes within the last year. (You want people who sold their homes in similar market conditions.) Call and ask them how they liked working with the agent and whether they'd do so again, what the agent's strengths and weaknesses are, and how long their homes were listed prior to sale.

A full list of these questions appears below. You can keep this list in front of you when you meet with each prospective agent, taking notes as you go. (You can also download this form from Nolo.com. For instructions, see "Get Updates, Checklists, Calculators, and More at Nolo.com" in the Introduction.)

Checklist: Questions to Ask Prospective Real Estate Agents

- ☐ How long have you been a real estate agent?
- ☐ Are you a Realtor (member of the National Board of Realtors)?
- ☐ Do you have a broker's license?
- ☐ Do you have any professional designations or have you taken any specialized courses?
- ☐ Will you provide me with a comparable market analysis?
- ☐ Are you available on a full-time basis?
- ☐ Would you ever represent me as a dual agent?
- ☐ How many residential real estate transactions have you been a part of in the last year?
- ☐ In how many transactions did you represent the seller?
- ☐ Do you specialize in a certain type of property?
- ☐ Do you specialize in a certain geographic area?
- ☐ How will I reach you?
- ☐ How would you prepare my home for sale?
- ☐ What was the difference between the list price and selling price of homes you sold in the last six months?
- ☐ How long did the houses you've sold in the last six months take to sell?
- ☐ How many buyers and sellers are you currently representing?
- ☐ How exactly would you market my property—and how is this superior to what other agents might do?
- ☐ Would you provide at least three names of recent clients who sold their homes with you in the last year and who will serve as references?

Making Your Agent-Client Relationship Official

Once you've found the agent you want to work with, you'll draw up a formal, written agreement. First, you may want to decide the commission percentage you'll pay. Then you can talk over some of the other details.

Negotiating the Agent's Commission

How much an agent charges is typically a matter of local custom, but as we've discussed, usually falls somewhere between 5% and 6% of the home's selling price. There's no set rule about this, however. Although some real estate agents may bristle when you try to negotiate a lower commission, there are several situations in which it makes sense:

- **You plan to do significant portions of the work yourself.** If you're going to take on an important part of the transaction that an agent would normally be expected to handle—creating your own website or showing the home to prospective purchasers, for example—you're justified in asking for a reduction in the commission.

- **You plan to use the same agent to sell and buy.** If you're going to use the same agent to sell this house and purchase your next one, it's worth asking the agent for a break (perhaps a percentage point off), knowing the agent will receive a commission on your purchase, too.

- **The agent ends up selling to an unrepresented buyer or a buyer represented by another agent in the same brokerage.** For reasons we've explained, you don't want an agent to attempt to represent both you and the buyer. But if the agent isn't paying a commission to another agent, part of that savings should be passed off to you. Similarly, if the agent sells through another agent in the same brokerage, the brokerage will come out ahead by collecting fees from both agents. It's fair for you to request a share of that savings.

Of course, no agent is going to accept a deal if there's hardly any money to be made on it, and the agent will have to get the managing broker's approval, too. On top of that, an agent agreeing to a reduced commission will have to either find a buyer's agent who is willing to take a reduced commission or take the entire reduction alone. The second option is the best one from your point of view; reducing the buyer's agent's commission can mean fewer prospective buyers coming to check your place out.

> **TIP**
>
> **Find out the commission split.** Your agent should tell you how he or she will split the commission with the buyer's agent: 50/50 is most common. However, some sellers' agents keep a bigger share of the pie, and that reduces the incentive for buyers' agents to show your home. If you're paying the standard commission where you live, make sure the buyer's agent gets at least half—if your agent doesn't volunteer the information or it doesn't appear in your listing contract, ask.

Signing a Listing Agreement

Once you and your agent have agreed on the commission amount, you're going to sign a "listing agreement": a contract that says that the agent has the right to list your house. It's important to understand the terms of this agreement, because you'll be bound by them—you won't, for example, be legally able to sneak off and make a side deal with a buyer that cuts out the agent's commission.

While the listing agreement is good for the agent, because it obligates you to work with him or her for a minimum amount of time, it also protects you, by explaining the agent's responsibilities and what you can do if he or she doesn't fulfill them.

After working out the commission amount (which will also be formalized in the agreement), you next must decide what kind of relationship you'll have with your agent. Your primary options are:

- **Exclusive right to sell.** This will probably be your agent's first choice: It gives the agent an exclusive right to sell your property for the duration of the agreement. Even if you find a buyer completely on your own, for instance, the friend of a friend whom you run into at the grocery store, you'll still have to pay your agent the full agreed-upon commission.

- **Exclusive agency.** This type of contract says that your agent is the only agent authorized to sell your house. But since you're not an agent, if you bring in the buyer yourself, you won't have to pay your agent's commission. This may sound like a good plan. But keep in mind that it reduces the agent's incentive to put time and effort into marketing your house—the agent knows that if you find a buyer first, his or her hard work will have been for nothing. And don't forget that you'll have to take care of all the follow-up work if the agent is no longer part of the deal.

- **Open listing.** With an open listing, you agree to pay a commission to whichever real estate agent brings in a buyer. Good luck. You'd end up in nearly the same position as a seller who isn't using an agent at all, because it's extremely unlikely than any one agent is going to try to market your property. Agents don't want to waste their time, knowing that if someone else ultimately finds a willing buyer for your house, that lucky agent will snag the commission.

Most listing agents use standard forms, created by state or local Realtor associations, to create the listing agreement. No surprise, these are generally written to protect the agent. So make sure it looks out for your interests as well and reflects what you talked over with your agent.

Here are some of the most important terms such an agreement will cover:

- **Duration.** Your listing agreement will last for a set amount of time. From your perspective, a shorter listing agreement is better. If you don't like the agent's services, you can easily walk away and choose a different agent. Of course, from the agent's perspective, a longer listing agreement is preferable, because the agent is going to do a lot of work to get the house ready to sell, and won't want to risk losing a commission just as it's starting to garner some real interest. Attorney Joel G. Kinney recommends 90-day listing agreements, explaining, "A lot of agents want six months, but if the house isn't moving, you want the option of trying a different listing agent or taking it off the market without interfering with the agreement with your agent." Ninety days should also be enough time for the listing agent to effectively market the property and make the sale. If you're happy with the agent's services at the end of the listing period, you can always renew the agreement.

- **Safety or protection clause.** Even though the contract has an expiration date, it will probably also include a clause that protects the agent or broker for a certain number of days after that date. This clause prevents you from trying to avoid paying an agent's commission by finding a buyer while you're represented by the agent, but waiting to conduct the sale to that buyer until your listing agreement has expired. (Sellers and buyers have been known to conspire, agreeing to sit tight until the listing agreement expires, then share the commission savings.) Make sure the clause has an exception making clear that it does not apply if you get a new agent when the listing contract ends (look for language like "void upon relisting"). Otherwise, if your new agent sells to someone that the first agent showed the property to, you could end up owing two commissions.

CAUTION

You may owe a commission on an offer you turn down! Most standard listing agreements say that the listing agent earns payment upon bringing in a buyer with an "acceptable" offer. If you receive a full-price offer but decide you're not going to sell (without having a legitimate reason), or even if the deal falls through, your listing agreement may obligate you to pay the commission. (A few states' courts reject this interpretation, however.) In any case, it's worth insisting that any such language in your listing agreement be changed to say that the agent earns a commission only if and when the sale closes, unless the closing was prevented by your (the seller's) conduct.

- **Duties.** The agreement may lay out the activities the agent is authorized to conduct on your behalf. Read through the list carefully, making sure you understand everything. If there are specific duties you want to require of the agent—for example, listing the property on the MLS, posting a yard sign, or creating a listing sheet—specify those as well.
- **Representations.** The agreement may also require you to verify certain facts—for instance, that you're in a legal position to sell the property and that to your knowledge no one else has an ownership interest in it.
- **Dispute resolution.** The agreement will probably specify how you will handle disputes that you can't work out informally, such as through mediation or binding arbitration.

Most standard contracts will include provisions that cover these issues. Don't sign without reading carefully, however—and don't be afraid to ask for any changes or amendments. Agents may resist changing their standard agreements, having used them many times in the past without incident. Nevertheless, if you're uncomfortable with something, there's no reason it can't be changed.

Small changes can be written right on the contract (make sure you get a copy), and large changes can be added with separate addendums that are referred to in the contract itself. (There's usually a space for additional terms; here you can refer to the addendum.)

TIP
After finding a great agent, listen to that person! Before selling her home, Carter asked a retired Realtor friend for her top piece of advice. "Listen to your Realtor," was the reply. "So I did," says Carter. "It wasn't always easy—for instance, I hadn't planned to spend $6,000 on pre-sale 'fluff and buff'—but that helped bring in a slew of offers over the list price. When you're a client, by definition you're doing something you don't do often and don't have expertise in. The eye the Realtor brings to a house is valuable and objective. Yet my retired friend said she was astonished at the number of clients whose approach was, 'I know better, and I'm not going to do that.'"

Hiring a Real Estate Attorney

In most states, you don't need a lawyer by your side in order to sell your house. However, in numerous states, such as Delaware, Hawaii, Massachusetts, and New York, real estate attorneys are a regular part of the homebuying process—or at the very least, the closing—either by law or by practice. To find out what role attorneys play in real estate transactions in your state, ask your agent or check with your state bar association or real estate commission.

Even in states where it isn't a legal requirement to hire an attorney when you buy a house, a complex transaction may need an attorney's assistance. Better to work with a lawyer to structure a deal, not salvage it. Depending on your needs and where you're selling a house, your attorney may become involved in one or more of the following tasks:

- negotiating, creating, or reviewing the sales contract
- overseeing the process to check for compliance with all terms and conditions of the contract
- helping you deal with issues that come up in the title search, such as an allegation that you failed to pay taxes or child support, and thus created liens or encumbrances on the property
- negotiating or representing you in a contract dispute with the buyer, and
- representing you at the closing.

An attorney can be especially important in complex house-sale transactions, such as the following:

- You own the house jointly with others.
- You're selling FSBO ("for sale by owner").
- You're not the homeowner, but an executor for an estate that is selling the house in probate.
- You have changed your mind about selling and need a legal reason to break the contract.
- The buyer is trying to get out of the deal, and you want to ensure that you can keep the escrow deposit.

Getting Recommendations for Excellent Real Estate Attorneys

To find potential attorneys, get recommendations from friends, coworkers, and trusted real estate professionals. If you plan to work with an attorney, be sure to use your own—the buyer's attorney cannot be expected to look after your legal interests.

Interview a few of the best prospects, asking about the attorney's experience helping residential home sellers, but also how much time the attorney spends on transactions similar to yours—especially if you're selling a condo or co-op.

Be sure to ask about the attorney's hourly rates or fees for services; expect to pay $150 to $350 per hour depending upon the services you need, and be sure to have a clear fee agreement. Attorneys who work solo rather than for a big firm are a viable option for you—the firepower of a large firm may be more than you need. But make sure the attorney truly has the degree of experience needed, and isn't just trying to fill up his or her slate of clients.

RESOURCE

Shop for real estate attorneys on Nolo's Lawyer Directory. Nolo's Lawyer Directory at www.nolo.com/lawyers offers comprehensive profiles of the lawyers who advertise there. You can also submit information about a particular legal issue to several local attorneys who handle real estate issues, and then pick the lawyer you'd like to work with.

Questions to Ask a Prospective Real Estate Attorney

When you meet with a prospective attorney, here are some questions to ask to make sure the attorney has the requisite experience and it's an otherwise good fit:

- **What percent of your time do you spend helping residential real estate sellers?** It's best to work with an attorney who spends 30% or more of the working day on transactions like yours.

- **How many years have you been handling residential real estate legal matters?** The longer the better, but at least two years. Someone just out of law school or another practice area may know almost nothing about a transaction like yours.

- **Do you charge hourly rates (if so, at what rate) or flat fees for services?** There's no one right answer—you'll want to compare fees between attorneys. But try not to base your decision solely on how high or low the fees are.

- **Are you a licensed and active member of the state bar association?** The only acceptable answer is "Yes." You want an attorney who's not only a bar member, but keeps up on the latest legal and practice matters.

- **Have you ever been subject to any bar association disciplinary proceedings or been sued for malpractice? What was the result?** Unless the outcomes were a complete dismissal or victory for the attorney, stay away from one who's gotten into hot water. (An Internet search for the lawyer's name and "disciplinary" or "malpractice" might turn up such information, too.)

- **How many individual home-selling clients have you represented in the past year?** A minimum of seven is best.

- **Would you provide the names of three recent clients who will serve as references?** Not all attorneys will provide references, for reasons of client confidentiality, but if one does, it's worth your time to follow up. Check whether the people you speak with were satisfied with the attorney's services and ask what it was like to work with the attorney.

A full list of these questions appears below. You can keep this list in front of you when you meet with each prospective attorney, taking notes as you go. (You can also download this form from Nolo.com. For instructions, see "Get Updates, Checklists, Calculators, and More at Nolo.com" in the Introduction.)

Checklist: Questions to Ask Prospective Attorneys

☐ What percent of your time do you spend helping residential real estate sellers?

☐ How many years have you been handling residential real estate legal matters?

☐ Do you charge hourly rates (if so, at what rate) or flat fees for services?

☐ Are you a licensed and active member of the state bar association?

☐ Have you ever been subject to any bar association disciplinary proceedings or been sued for malpractice? What was the result?

☐ How many individual home-selling clients have you represented in the past year?

☐ Would you provide the names of three recent clients who will serve as references?

Hiring a Tax Expert for Advice on Your Home Sale

If you turn a profit on the sale of your home, you might be worried about owing capital gains taxes to Uncle Sam. The reality is, however, that many taxpayers will not owe tax on capital gains resulting from the sale of the home. This is due to something called the "principal residence exclusion" (you can get details in IRS Publication 523, *Selling Your Home*, available at www.irs.gov).

In a nutshell, explains Katy Ayer, a CPA in Arroyo Grande, California, "If it is a simple home sale, meaning you owned and lived in your house as your principal residence for more than two of the immediately preceding five years, and the total gain on the sale of your home is less than $250,000 ($500,000 if you are married filing jointly), you can probably handle the tax reporting on your own." However, for anything more complicated, you will want the help of a tax professional. Katy Ayer provides the following examples of complicating factors:

- the home was previously used for business or rented out
- the home was acquired via inheritance or transfer between family members or divorcing spouses
- a taxpayer and spouse are combining formerly separate households and trying to determine how the exclusion will work for them
- the seller (or the seller's spouse) has already sold a principal residence within the preceding two years, or
- the taxpayer does not meet the standards for the full exclusion, but may be eligible for a reduced exclusion due to a job change, change in family situation, or illness.

These are the most common situations, but as Katy Ayer notes, "There are many others, and it never hurts to run your situation by a tax adviser, even for an apparently straightforward home sale."

Finding and Choosing a Top-Notch Accountant or Tax Pro

If you have any questions about possible tax issues with your home sale, get advice from a tax pro when you first start thinking about selling your home. (Also consider having this pro prepare your next tax return.)

Heading to your corner tax franchise chain or basic "tax preparer" may not be wise in this situation. As attorney and Nolo author Stephen Fishman explains, "The largest tax preparation firm is H & R Block, but many mom-and-pop operations open for business in storefront offices during tax time. Tax preparers are largely unlicensed and unregulated. They are generally not a good choice for tax advice or tax planning, or preparing anything other than the simplest tax returns." Instead, you should speak to either an "enrolled agent" (EA), a "certified public accountant" (CPA), or (in especially complex situations) a tax attorney before you sell your home.

Enrolled agents are tax advisers as well as preparers. They've either gained five years of experience or passed a tough exam and obtained a license from the IRS. They tend to be the most affordable type of tax professional. An experienced EA can give you solid advice when you sell your home.

CPAs, too, must pass a difficult exam (after a lengthy training program) and obtain state licensing. CPAs represent the high end of the spectrum—they are generally the most knowledgeable and expensive of the various tax pros. In addition to preparing tax returns, they perform sophisticated accounting and tax work. CPAs are found in large national firms (used primarily by large businesses) as well as small local outfits. Some states also license public accountants. These professionals are competent but not as highly regarded as CPAs.

Tax attorneys are, as their name implies, attorneys who specialize in tax law. They typically focus on litigation with the IRS and other tax agencies, rather than providing the type of tax-planning and return-preparation services you need when selling your home. But if you're already working with an attorney on a related matter, such as planning your estate, the attorney may be able to help work out a tax strategy that fits your goals.

As always, we advise starting by getting recommendations from friends, colleagues, and your real estate agent. If you don't come up with any good options, check with the National Association of Enrolled Agents (www.naea.org) or a local CPA society. Talk with at least three tax professionals before choosing one to consult with.

Questions to Ask a Prospective Tax Pro

When you meet with a prospective tax professional, here are some questions to ask to make sure the person has the requisite credentials and experience for what you need.

- **Do you have a PTIN (preparer tax identification number)?** Anyone who prepares tax returns for money must have a valid PTIN issued by the IRS. Don't hire someone who doesn't have one.
- **How many years' experience do you have advising on tax matters?** The longer the better, but at least two years.

- **Are you familiar with the tax aspects of residential real estate transactions?** Many tax pros specialize—for example, some prepare only business tax returns. You're best off with a tax pro who routinely deals with residential real estate transactions, including preparing returns. Handling residential real estate sales is a common tax issue, so you should have no difficulty finding a tax pro with plenty of experience in this area.

- **How do you set your fee?** It's best to pose the question of fees this way, rather than asking, "How much do you charge?" It's impossible for a tax pro to give you an exact answer about how much the fee will be until the work is completed. Some tax pros charge by the hour; others charge a standard fee for each tax form they prepare; still others use both methods. Ask for a fee schedule.

- **What type of licensing and credentials do you have?** As explained above, you're looking for either an EA or a CPA, not a mere tax preparer.

- **Have you ever been subject to any disciplinary proceedings?** What was the result? Steer clear of anyone who's gotten into trouble. If the tax pro is a CPA, contact your state's board of accountancy to check whether any disciplinary action has been taken against him or her. If the person is an enrolled agent, you can ask the IRS Office of Professional Responsibility whether he or she has been disciplined. An Internet search for the person's name and "disciplinary" might turn such information up, too.

- **Will you sign my tax return after preparing it?** Any tax pro who prepares your return for compensation is required by the IRS to sign the return. Don't deal with any supposed professional who refuses to do so—it means the person has something to hide.

- **Will you help me if my return is audited or questioned by the IRS?** If the IRS audits you or sends you a letter, will the tax pro be available to help you? Will he or she represent you before the IRS? What additional fees will be charged for such help? This is important follow-up.

- **Would you provide the names of three recent clients who will serve as references?** Not all tax professionals will provide references, for reasons of client confidentiality, but if one does, it's worth your time to follow up. Also check online resources such as Yelp for reviews.

A full list of these questions appears below. You can keep this list in front of you when you meet with each prospective tax pro, taking notes as you go. (You can also download this form from Nolo.com. For instructions, see "Get Updates, Checklists, Calculators, and More at Nolo.com" in the Introduction.)

Checklist: Questions to Ask Prospective Tax Pros

☐ Do you have a PTIN (preparer tax identification number)?

☐ How many years' experience do you have advising on tax matters?

☐ Are you familiar with the tax aspects of residential real estate transactions?

☐ How do you set your fee?

☐ What type of licensing and credentials do you have?

☐ Have you ever been subject to any disciplinary proceedings? What was the result?

☐ Will you sign my tax return after preparing it?

☐ Will you help me if my return is audited or questioned by the IRS?

☐ Would you provide the names of three recent clients who will serve as references?

Prep Work: Preinspections, Repairs, and Improvements

When was the last time anyone took a comprehensive look at your house's condition—the whole house, including any crawl space or attic? Unless you've had major remodeling done, your answer is most likely "Not since we bought the place." That's when most homeowners hire an inspector to write up a report. Since that time, you've no doubt fixed and replaced a few things, overlooked some minor problems, and possibly been blissfully ignorant about a few others. The trouble is, what seems like a minor or non-issue to you now may turn into a major negotiating point in the hands of a buyer.

The degree to which buyers ask for repairs and price reductions is largely market driven. In a hot market, they'll hardly care. But back during the market downturn, buyers and their agents learned to be ruthless, demanding repairs or money for practically every problem that turned up in a home inspection. Dripping faucets and a tear in the screen door became ways to get more cash out of the seller. If your local market isn't among those that have become superheated lately, some of that spirit may remain—and supply ample reason for you to find out what needs fixing, and possibly fix it, before you put the house on the market.

TIP

The longer you've been in a house, the more problems may have sprung up without your noticing. Paul A. Rude, an experienced home inspector in California explains, "Commonly, people have no idea that the roof is worn out and pipes and wires have deteriorated, especially in an older house. It doesn't mean the owner has done anything wrong, it's just that houses age. Another issue that can be painful is when the owner spent money upgrading the house and there's something wrong with the work— like a defect or code violation. These can be expensive to fix."

Even in hot markets, buyers who haven't thrown all caution to the wind will likely make their offer contingent on having the house professionally inspected and the buyer approving the results. By the time they're conducting inspections, you will have most likely filled out and provided a complete set of written disclosures (described in Chapter 4), which warned the seller about any problems with the house (within your knowledge, that is). These disclosures will go a long way toward reducing the surprise factor.

The key thing to realize is that unpleasant surprises, no matter how small, can sour the mood between buyers and sellers. Even if the buyer doesn't ask for a price reduction, he or she may suspect that you were trying to hide something. "When buyers do inspections and turn up problems, it's always a big deal. A tipping point," says California Realtor Ira Serkes. "The buyer may get more hard-nosed on credits or price reductions, and may even walk away then."

So, to make sure your house is in the best possible condition and can be priced accordingly—or that a buyer can't turn to hard-line negotiations with you when problems are discovered during the post-offer inspection—do a preinspection yourself, and consider hiring a professional home inspector to find out what condition your property is *really* in. This chapter will cover what you realistically can or should do.

Root It Out: Inspect It Yourself

In Chapter 1, we discussed fixing obvious and easily dealt with problems in your home. Now take an even harder look, surveying your property for other problems that might be an issue for prospective buyers. Check into the following:

- Do the heating, air conditioning, and water heater work?
- Do appliances that will be included in the home sale function properly?
- Do all light fixtures and electrical outlets work properly? Are there burnt out bulbs or exposed wire?
- Are any flooring and baseboards loose or damaged?
- Are cabinets and doors properly hung; and do sliding doors, screens, latches, and locks function correctly?
- Do the roof and windows have leaks?
- Are cracks evident in the ceiling or walls?

- Is there any water damage to walls, floors, or outside structures?
- Do any faucets leak?
- Do the toilets run properly?
- Is mold or mildew growing anywhere?
- Are smoke detectors and carbon monoxide detectors installed and in working order?

Discovering problems doesn't necessarily mean you need to fix them—whether you do so is a matter of resources and strategy. If you had unlimited time and resources, you could fix everything and the buyer would never see the problems. But if the list is long or will cost more than you can afford right now, do some prioritizing with your real estate agent. (If the house is in really bad shape, you might simply advertise it as a "fixer upper," as discussed later in this chapter.)

TIP
Keep manuals, warranties, and repair records for the buyer.
Don't recycle or toss product manuals or warranties for your home appliances and mechanical systems, such as the water heater, built-in microwave, irrigation system, and burglar alarm. Set them aside for your buyer. (Or if you've already lost them, print out new ones from online sources such as www.manualsonline.com.) Also pull together records of what's been done on the house. That lets the buyer know, for example, how long ago an item was replaced, or who to call for follow-up work or repairs.

Hiring a Professional Home Inspector

If you're serious about making sure your house is in pristine condition, consider hiring a home inspector next. Don't get confused—this isn't the same person whom the buyer will hire to look at the house later. Instead, this is a pro who works for you, helping identify hidden problems.

Lesson learned the hard way **I should've had the house inspected before listing it.** "With my children grown, I decided to move to Manhattan," says Susan. "I found a great deal on a co-op, and closed on it. But now I was paying two mortgages, and had to quickly sell my 120-year-old, five-bedroom home in suburban New Jersey. A contractor who'd done extensive remodeling work on the place said it was in good shape, so I thought 'How convenient, no need to get a separate inspection.' The house showed beautifully, it was in a desirable neighborhood, and it brought in a terrific offer soon after I put it on the market. Then the buyer's inspection report came in. It said the house needed $100,000 worth of foundation repairs. The buyers got cold feet and pulled out, and I took the house off the market to fix the foundation. Although the actual repairs cost only $15,000, having the property off the market for a month tainted it in the eyes of prospective buyers. The next offer was $35,000 less than the original one. Had I arranged a professional inspection before listing, I could have saved thousands of dollars, not to mention time and aggravation."

Unless you're a contractor or building professional, you simply won't be equipped to find anything but the more superficial or visible issues. By contrast, qualified home inspectors are typically contractors or other professionals who have specific knowledge in all aspects of home construction, including plumbing, wiring, and more.

In some parts of the U.S., real estate agents routinely get a professional inspection done on every house they're preparing for sale. Even in areas where it's less common, listing agents may recommend to clients whose homes show signs of needing major structural work that they get a professional inspection done, to head off those nasty surprises.

As a middle-ground solution, an experienced agent may be able to point out repair needs that you didn't notice. (But the agent can't be expected to do some things that an inspector would, such as climb a ladder into your roof space to check for rodent infestation or dry rot.)

To find a good inspector, ask friends as well as your real estate agent for recommendations, examine each inspector's sample reports, and make sure the inspector is licensed (if that's required in your state) and is a member of the American Society of Home Inspectors or ASHI (www.ashi.org).

But ... If the Inspector Finds It, Don't You Have to Tell the Buyers About It?

True, there's a flip side to doing all this inspecting: In most states, you have a legal duty to disclose known defects to your prospective buyer (as we'll discuss more in Chapter 4). And the more you know about, the more you have to disclose. Some sellers therefore balk at doing a preinspection, preferring to have their disclosures look clean, and ignoring any hidden problems until they're in contract with a prospective buyer.

But remember, the buyer is likely to have a separate inspection done anyway. And unless the buyer happens to choose a completely incompetent inspector, the same repair issues are likely to be revealed. At that point, you're at a psychological and negotiating disadvantage. If the deal falls through, turning around and putting the house back on the market will cost you time and money, which might lead you to cave in to repair requests anyway.

What You Can Ask Home Inspectors to Do

For around $250–$800, the inspector will identify problems with the home, such as leaks in the roof, possible water damage, remodeling efforts that don't meet current building codes, and improperly grounded outlets. With this information, the home inspector will prepare a written report and may make repair recommendations. If the report gives your house the equivalent of an A grade, you can hand copies of the report to buyers, to show them what great shape the place is in. (They may still get their own inspections done, but it provides a professional counterbalance to any negative information that might turn up.)

Apart from the general inspection, various specialized types of inspections are available, the most notable being for pests (such as termites, carpenter ants, and dry rot). While some inspectors (usually depending on local custom) mix the pest inspection into the general inspection, these are really two different specialties. Someone who knows foundations doesn't necessarily know termites. So for the most comprehensive inspections, hire two or more different inspectors.

TIP
You may need to give the buyer a pest inspection report anyway. In some areas of the U.S., lenders routinely ask to see the results of a pest inspection before they fund the loan. And although it's the buyer who needs the loan, local custom may dictate that the seller pay for the pest inspection. A local real estate professional can tell you what the practice is where you live.

You can also hire inspectors who deal with specialized issues, like home energy assessments, the condition of your home's soil grading, a boathouse or other unusual structure, or amenities like a hot tub or swimming pool. But unless you suspect a problem that you're worried a buyer will want to negotiate, you'll probably be fine just hiring a general inspector and perhaps a pest inspector and letting the buyer decide what other specialists to bring in.

If the cost or hassle of a full inspection is more than you think necessary, hire an inspector who is willing to do a more basic review for less money. Some are willing to do a simple walk-through with a home seller, at an hourly rate. (Look for one who's been a general contractor.) It's less comprehensive than a full inspection, and the inspector won't draw up a written report afterward—you'll need to take your own notes—but the inspector will alert you to the major issues.

A good inspector will point out which of the home's defects are likely to scare buyers the most and should top the repair list. Examples might include electrical problems, which buyers tend to assume (not always correctly) are a fire hazard, or gutters hanging off, which look shabby. Neither of these is terribly expensive to fix.

Preparing for the Inspector's Visit

You and any co-owners should be present when the inspector comes, especially if you're not going to get a written report. This ensures you retain as much of the information the inspector shares as possible, and are able to ask any questions.

You'll get the most from the inspection if you're well prepared. Here's what to do before the inspector arrives:

- **Create a list of issues upon which you'd like the inspector's opinion.** Even the best home inspectors won't look at each of the hundreds of components of your home. So if there's something you're curious about, like why a light switch won't turn on, bring it to the inspector's attention.
- **Clear any entry and access points.** If there's stuff piled in front of the crawl space entrance or you've forgotten how to open the attic trapdoor, you'll miss your chance to have the inspector examine these areas. (But you can be sure that the buyer will later demand that they be opened up.) Even closets should be cleared out, especially if they're so full it's impossible to access them. Also make sure the inspector can get to the electrical panel.
- **Reread the inspector's contract or brochure.** If you're not sure what's included in the inspection, clarify this with the inspector during the visit. For example, many inspectors won't examine the security system, which you might want to have separately looked at if you suspect a problem.

To Fix or Not to Fix?

Having done your own inspections, and possibly hired an inspector to give you a written or oral report, you now have two choices: You can correct some or all of the identified problems, or you can lower your house's sale price to account for them.

★ *B*est thing we ever did **Listen to our agent's fix-up suggestions.** "We were lucky to find an energetic agent with years of experience," says Stephen. "She helped point out issues we didn't even know were fixable, and then found solutions. For instance, our furnace intake vent was covered with an old, wooden bench-like structure—obviously homemade, in bad shape, and cluttering up the living room. She found someone who could craft a beautiful insert to match our hardwood floors. Wish we'd gotten that advice years ago!"

What Repairs to Make Right Away

Even in hot markets where problems might be overlooked, buyers are especially drawn to a house that's been attentively cared for, unmarred by a single loose drawer pull or creaking hinge. That's why you'll often see the words "move-in ready" or "lovingly maintained" in real estate ads—as opposed to phrases like "needs some TLC." (Surveys show that the vast majority of buyers are looking for homes that are move-in ready.)

💡 TIP

Live in a planned neighborhood or development? You'll have to work even harder to make sure that your house stands apart from the rest—especially if a number of nearby, similar-looking homes are for sale. Showing that your house has been well cared for can make a big difference.

Doing repairs ahead of time is often a no-brainer if they offer a big bang for your buck—in other words, they won't take major time or money, but will either make the house look much better, or save buyers from shock reactions as in, "Ew, do we have to deal with that?"

Another reason to do repairs ahead of time is that you'll have more control over how they're carried out, and may be able to save some money as a result. For example, while a buyer who discovers loose roof tiles might demand that you hire a professional to replace them, if you can replace them in advance yourself, the buyer may never know there was a problem.

Repairs You Can Probably Handle

Here are some repairs that many people can handle if comfortable using basic tools:

- painting
- coating outdoor woodwork, such as decks, landscaping, pruning trees, and planting new flowers
- replacing lightbulbs, switchplates, and similar items
- clearing gutters (if the roof isn't too high) and outdoor drains
- changing filters in heating systems
- adjusting or replacing hardware on doors, windows, and cabinets, and
- making basic fence repairs.

The following repairs require more skill, but are still relatively easy with a little advice from a local hardware or home supply store:

- fixing or replacing dripping or otherwise nonfunctional faucets and valves (in many cases, you can turn off the water, remove the item, and take it to a home supply store or plumbing supply house to make sure you get the right parts)
- replacing locks and other hardware on doors
- replacing broken sash cords on windows
- replacing broken parts of irrigation systems
- making minor repairs of concrete sidewalks and masonry
- repairing gates
- adding or replacing spark screens on chimneys, and
- recaulking seams in bathroom floors, around plumbing fixtures, and on the home's exterior.

The one area not to touch is electrical work, unless you're trained in it! The chance of making a mistake that could hurt someone or burn the house down is too big to risk.

Finally, making repairs now means you'll have fewer problems to disclose to the buyer. If your list of disclosures was getting long, this can make the deal look cleaner. (Keep in mind, however, that you may need to disclose the history of a problem even after it's been repaired. But this tends to be true only for issues that might recur, such as water seepage.) We'll discuss disclosure requirements further in Chapter 4.

> **CAUTION**
>
> **Don't ignore problems you find during your preliminary inspection.** Most state's disclosure laws require you to disclose problems you know about, so the worst possible strategy would be to investigate your house's repair needs but then neither repair them nor tell the buyer about them. If you're not willing to put in the work or notify the buyer, you're better off skipping preinspections altogether.

If you're comfortable handling minor or basic repairs yourself but need a little guidance, look at online websites like www. thisoldhouse.com, www.diynetwork.com, or www.lowes.com. These provide basic "how-to" videos and instructions. If you're not equipped to take on these tasks yourself, don't! Evidence of inadequate repair work can turn off buyers as much as the original problem would. A general repair person may be able to tackle basic repairs for a low cost.

Factoring Unrepaired Problems Into Your House Price

Sometimes it's not worth doing a repair before putting a house on the market. Major repairs, in particular, like fixing a crack in the foundation, can be expensive, disrupt your life, and may not even help your bottom line (that is, you won't get $30,000 more for your house because you spent $30,000 repairing the foundation). And the problems may be just plain bigger than you're financially able to handle—for example, if the house needs extensive masonry work on its wraparound brick porch.

In such cases, you may be better off having one or two contractors take a look and estimate the cost of repair, then lowering the sale price accordingly. Ask for written estimates for the needed work.

You'd then tell prospective buyers that the issue exists and that you accounted for the repair cost in the sale price. If a buyer says, "I'll pay $10,000 less because there are pieces of defective siding," you can comfortably respond (through your agent) with something like, "I told you about the siding in the disclosures, and factored it into the market value of the property. It should cost about $2,500 to replace those few pieces, and I listed the house at $3,000 below market value to compensate for that and for any inconvenience to the buyer." Back this up by giving the buyer copies of the written estimates.

Even minor repairs and cosmetic improvements can be left undone in a very hot market. If your primary motivation is to get the house sold and move on, why slow the process down? You might make some buyers very happy by allowing them to strengthen their purchase offer by promising to take the house without requesting that you repair any of the disclosed problems.

Skipping All Repairs: Selling "As Is"

Some sellers who don't want to deal with the hassle of identifying or fixing problems may consider selling their homes "as is." This essentially says to the buyer, "Here's my house and here's my price; don't expect me to fix anything or lower the price for repairs." If you're in an area where many investors are buying up properties (for fixing up or renting out), they're an especially likely audience for an as-is property.

You can't completely wash your hands of responsibility, however. Not even an as-is sale relieves you of your duty to disclose the problems you know about. And some buyers will still insist on an inspection contingency in the contract, reasoning that they want to know what the house's problems are before they make a commitment to buy, even if you're not going to fix them. (And remember, with such a contingency, a buyer who doesn't approve the results of the inspection can back out entirely.)

Although an as-is sale may simplify the sales process, it probably won't help you net as much as you could have for your home. Interested buyers will expect you to offer a rock-bottom price, to compensate for the risk they're assuming. If there's a major problem with the house, they know it falls largely on them to deal with it.

If you live in an area with a good number of as-is, low-priced properties, including foreclosures and bank-owned homes, your profit may be further reduced if you also try to sell as-is. Some buyers will be tired of seeing fixer-uppers (especially if the others are in really bad shape) and bypass yours. Other buyers will expect your price to be comparable to the prices on these deeply discounted homes. You might be better off fixing up your house and selling it at market value.

> **TIP**
>
> **Don't stop at the fix-ups.** As we'll discuss in the next chapter, savvy home sellers take further steps toward making their homes look gorgeous, by cleaning, decluttering, and adding decorative touches.

What About Remodels or Home Improvements?

Now let's consider a situation where your house doesn't necessarily need repairs, but is just tired, outdated, or outmoded. A remodel might make it much more saleable—but will also cost big bucks. What's your best course of action?

The first thing to realize is that not all home improvements are created equal. Some will increase the value of your home, and some will actually make selling more difficult. Below, we'll discuss how to tell the difference.

Time is also a factor, of course. When was the last time you heard about a remodeling project that didn't finish late and over budget? Still, if you're reading this well in advance of your proposed sale date—and are sitting in a cramped kitchen that's just begging to have a wall torn down and new countertops put in—then keep reading.

TIP

Some buyers are looking for a home that they can fix up to their tastes. A home in need of a remodel—and priced accordingly—offers buyers a chance to customize it. Why should they pay extra for your new granite countertops if they were eager to use recycled glass? One useful guideline: If the house looks so grim that it will be hard for buyers to imagine how it would look after a remodel, you might be better off doing some of the work ahead of time.

Projects With the Highest Resale Value

If you're willing to take on a remodeling project, don't waste time on ones that won't raise buyers' interest levels enough to offset the cost and then some. The following projects have been shown to have the highest financial impact when selling a home:

- **Kitchens.** People like to see modern conveniences and styles in the kitchen. Especially in older homes, kitchen improvements tend to add serious value. Just read the real estate ads—you'll notice how many highlight updated kitchen features.
- **Bathrooms.** Second to kitchen remodels in raising your selling price are bathroom remodels. Again, modernizing older styles or appliances usually results in good return, as does adding a new bathroom.
- **Attic additions.** Any time you can turn dead space into functional space, you're likely to see a good return, as well as make your home interesting to a larger pool of buyers.
- **Outdoor improvements.** Your house makes a first impression quickly, so sprucing up its outdoor appearance is a smart investment. This includes siding (fiber cement tends to cost the most, but has the best return) and landscaping, particularly in the front yard. Adding a wooden deck is a great way to add value, too.
- **Roofs and windows.** These are expensive to replace, and buyers expect them to be in good condition. Unfortunately, that means that while replacing them won't dramatically increase resale value, not replacing them could significantly decrease it.

Best thing we ever did **Left the roof replacement to the buyers.** "This may go against conventional wisdom," says Aileen, "but we were in a hurry to sell, and the roof—while it was due for replacement—didn't actually look bad, and wasn't yet leaking. We made sure the rest of our house looked great. A number of buyers fell in love with the place, and we ended up selling to one who not only made the top offer, but specifically waived the roof repair issue!"

Projects That Can Negatively Affect Resale Value

Almost any project has the potential to negatively affect your home's selling value. A general rule is that the more personal your choices, the less likely they are to have a positive effect on sale value. You'll need to keep a close eye on current trends, and follow them in a way that's most likely to please everyone without turning anyone off.

Here are the types of projects to avoid, if your main goal is to maximize your home's selling price.

- **Luxury upgrades.** While no one wants to see the absolute cheapest renovations in a home, top-quality upgrades often don't have the return of mid-range ones, unless you're in a very high-end home. Marble floors in the bathroom or custom cabinets in the kitchen may be nice, but don't assume buyers will pay proportionately for these luxuries.
- **Rooms that don't fit with the floor plan.** Converting the back patio to a family room may be a perfect way to add more space to your home, but if your dining room window now looks into the family room, it probably won't be well-loved by buyers.
- **Garage conversions.** These can give homeowners much-needed space, but many buyers like having garages, too, so converting this space usually won't increase value.
- **A swimming pool.** A pool may seem like the ultimate luxury to you—but it can actually be more of a hindrance to selling than a help. Parents with small children may view a pool as a safety hazard and some people would rather enjoy a yard full of greenery than one filled with a concrete pool. Consider also

whether it's usable for most of the year. While a pool may be a selling point in parts of Florida and California (though that's less true in the current drought), it could be a serious liability in Minnesota or Wisconsin.

RESOURCE
Learn more about how much you can expect to recoup given current buyer perceptions. See Remodeling Online's "Cost vs. Value Report" at www.remodeling.hw.net.

Big-Picture Factors That Affect Resale Value

Even if you do the right kind of projects, achieving a high return on your investment also depends on other factors—in particular, your surrounding neighborhood and how dramatic the changes to all or part of your house will be. Before coming to any conclusions about whether an improvement is likely to add value, consider the following.

Turning your house into the fanciest one in the neighborhood can backfire. If you live in a neighborhood of two-bedroom bungalows and you add a second story to put in a couple of extra bedrooms, you may not see a high return. Buyers looking for homes of that size won't be looking in your area. On the other hand, if it's a hot neighborhood or many of your neighbors are making similar improvements (perhaps because these affordable homes are on large lots and in a great school district), you might fare well doing the same. And if you're simply bringing your house up to neighborhood standards, that too may be a worthwhile project.

Upgrades to a newer home probably won't have the same impact that they would in an older home. In a 1950s home, an original kitchen will likely make buyers think: "I guess we'll start with a kitchen remodel!" The same isn't necessarily true of a house that's just a few years old, which means you're less likely to increase a newer home's value significantly by remodeling.

Your upgrades should be in sync with the rest of the house. Focusing narrowly on only one room—creating the perfect master suite, for example—can be a mistake. If the rest of your house was last updated 30 years ago, it will look even shabbier in comparison to the upgraded suite. A similar mistake is to put a sleek new appliance, such as a stainless steel refrigerator or a wine cooler, into an otherwise tired and dated kitchen. On the flip side, if you've updated everything but one bedroom, which still has old wallpaper and carpet, it will stick out like a sore thumb. Even a small investment to replace the wallpaper and carpet might have a huge impact, making the room fit in with everything else.

Spending on a high-end home will yield the best returns. From a practical perspective, you shouldn't expect to recover as much from improvements to a modestly priced home as you would for improvements to a high-end one. Spending $30,000 to remodel a kitchen with top-of-the-line appliances in a home that costs $150,000 won't have nearly the return the same remodel would in an $800,000 home.

A final thought on choosing which improvements, if any, to make: You'll get the most for your money if the improvements are visible to buyers. For example, while upgrading electrical wiring in an older home makes it safer and therefore more desirable, it doesn't excite buyers' imaginations. But a remodeled kitchen or new hardwood flooring is right before their eyes, looking great. ●

Telling Buyers What You Know: Disclosure Laws

Most—though not all—American states require a home seller to fill out and give a buyer a written report detailing the property's various features and disclosing any known material defects and hazards. In many states, the law actually includes the precise wording that must go into the standard seller disclosure form.

Even in states with no disclosure law, providing written disclosures has become common practice. Sellers often use a form prepared by the state's real estate agents' association. As Nancy Atwood, a real estate broker in Massachusetts (which has no disclosure law) describes it, "If home sellers don't go ahead and provide a disclosure form, most buyers will think they've got something to hide."

Not to delve too deep into legal history here, but it's worth understanding that these disclosure laws represent a major change from an old legal standard called *caveat emptor*, or buyer beware. That basically meant that if buyers didn't ask about or discover the issue, tough luck—the seller was under no obligation to say anything. Shades of that old standard remain in some parts of the United States.

TIP

Some types of sellers don't need to provide disclosures. If you've never actually lived in the home (for instance, because you inherited it) or been responsible for it (not even as a landlord), your state's law probably exempts you from preparing disclosures. Double-check with your real estate agent or an attorney.

Assuming you don't qualify for an exception to your state's disclosure law, plan to carefully and accurately fill out your seller disclosure form. It's a sufficiently important part of the process that we've devoted this whole chapter to it. Done correctly, seller disclosures can foster mutual understanding about the transaction and increase the buyer's comfort level. Done badly, they can lead to bad feelings and contentious negotiations during the transaction and possibly lawsuits later.

TIP

No need to disclose what you don't know. You are responsible for disclosing only information within your personal knowledge. In other words, you don't usually need to hire inspectors to turn up problems you never had an inkling existed. But turning a blind eye to problems that any reasonable person could have seen won't cut it.

What's on the Typical State Disclosure Form

Disclosure forms vary from state to state, but are most often laid out as a sort of checklist. You'll likely need to answer yes or no questions about, or check off boxes indicating the existence of, various features of the property and possibly conditions surrounding or affecting it.

In some cases, the information requested on the form is simply a statement of fact, such as what year your house was built in, whether your water source is private or public, and whether all your plumbing and drains connect to the sewer system. In other cases, you may be asked to rate or describe the condition of various items (from the furnace to the dishwasher to the roof) or to indicate cases where you simply don't know the answer.

Because there's a lot to cover, the typical form breaks the disclosures down into categories. In Colorado, for example, the main categories on the disclosure form are "Improvements" (covering structural conditions; roof; electrical and telecommunications; mechanical, water, sewer, and other utilities; and "other") and "General" (covering use, zoning, and legal issues; access, parking, drainage, and signage; water and sewer supply; environmental conditions; common interest or community association property; and "other").

Some states' disclosure forms are more comprehensive than others. For example, some drill into issues like legal disputes concerning the property (such as boundary encroachments), past meth lab usage, existing zoning violations (such as a use of the property that doesn't conform to local law), or community association fees. Some require information about suicides, murders, and other deaths on the property, nearby criminal activity, or other factors, such as excessive neighborhood noise.

A real estate professional in your area, or the state department of real estate, should be able to tell you about the disclosure law in your state and provide the proper form. Also see the Real Estate area of Nolo's website; the "Selling a House" page contains guides to filling out the disclosure form in selected states.

How Far Should You Go in Disclosing?

Some sellers simply fill out the form and call it a day, but this isn't necessarily the best approach. You may know about issues that the form doesn't cover, or wonder whether a particular question "really" requires you to disclose a particular issue. When in doubt, it's ordinarily best to avoid the potential for liability and tell all. Although it goes against some sellers' instincts, full disclosure of all property defects offers a number of advantages.

First, giving buyers a full picture of the property's condition will help increase their confidence that you're dealing fairly. That leads to smoother negotiations all the way up to the closing day.

Second, full disclosure increases the likelihood that your home will ultimately sell for the price offered. Even in a hot market, a buyer whose offer you've accepted knows that you're not going to be eager to re-list the home, and that you therefore have an interest in taking the deal all the way to closing. The buyer may, therefore, negotiate for price reductions or money for repairs or related issues during the escrow period, particularly as inspections turn up home defects. "It's less common now as the market has heated up, but I've seen home inspector advertisements to home buyers saying that they can help bring your contract price down," says David Wangsness, an agent with Coldwell Banker Bain Associates in Bellevue, Washington. Such tactics can shave thousands, or even tens of thousands of dollars off the price you thought the buyers were going to pay.

Your listing agent can, however, make it very difficult for buyers to chip away at the purchase price based on something they already knew about through your disclosures. California Realtor Ira Serkes says, "My first question would be, 'Why is this coming up now?' In fact, we've by then ideally given the buyers enough information that they not only knew of the existence of the problem, but knew its extent, and how much it will cost to fix. That makes it harder for them to come back saying, 'Our contractor says this job will cost $35,000' when all our estimates showed much less."

Disclosing what you know will additionally protect you from legal problems in the coming days or even years (discussed under "Legal Liability If You Disobey State Disclosure Laws," below.)

Lesson learned the hard way

Don't hide problems from potential buyers. "My now ex-husband and I had for years noticed a slight mildew smell in our home's family room," says Madeline. "When we put the home on the market, my ex insisted that we play dumb instead of doing a preinspection. We accepted an offer and, when it came time for the buyers' inspections, said they had to be conducted in the afternoon. We aired out the family room in the morning to let the smell dissipate. Sure enough, the buyers discovered that the house had a mold problem anyway. They forwarded the inspector's report to our agent and demanded a $40,000 discount on the home price. The word from our agent was that the buyers were pretty ticked off and would not back down on the $40,000. We knew that if we fell out of contract we'd have to disclose the report to any future interested buyers, so we ended up knocking $40,000 off the home price."

Where do you enter an issue that doesn't seem to fit anywhere on the form? You'll probably notice various "other" boxes, specifically meant to encourage broad disclosures and to cover issues that weren't already named. For example, if your community's groundwater has become contaminated by nearby underground fracking, the fact that no specific box for this exists on your disclosure form would not excuse you from mentioning it in the "other" box.

Or, if a violent crime occurred on your property such that buyers might be dismayed to learn about it, better to disclose that, too. You don't have to tell buyers about every little burglary or car break-in, but if a crime was horrific enough that your property may be considered "stigmatized"—for example, if neighbors point to it and say, "That's the house where …"—you should mention it. Your buyer is likely to find out about it someday, and it's better if it comes from you.

> **TIP**
>
> **Calling in the Ghostbusters—for real?!** Don't laugh, but some sellers offer to have a priest, a New Age healer, or a feng shui specialist come and bless the house, burn sage, or do whatever it takes to clear it of negative energies. Hey, if it helps sell your house….

The broadness of most states' disclosure requirements does not, however, mean you have to mention every little bend in your Venetian blinds or scratch on the floor. State-required disclosures are typically limited to "material" defects or hazards. What's meant by "material?" It's something that would have an impact on the value of the property, a buyer's decision to purchase it, or an owner's use of the property.

If you're spending any time wondering, "Is this a material defect or not?" then you're probably best off disclosing the matter. Buyers won't be put off by these minor issues—they'll more likely appreciate being given a full picture of what's going on in the home. (Remember, the mere fact that a problem or defect exists doesn't mean you must repair or correct it—unless it's a basic health and safety issue, in which case either the buyer's lender or insurance company may refuse to let the deal go through until it's fixed.)

> **Best thing we ever did**
>
> **Disclose everything and more.** "We had so many problems with our house in the mountains," says Wren, "I figured anything I held back from prospective buyers was bound to come back and bite us. I told buyers about the mudslide, the septic tank problems, and even what a pain it was taking care of the hot tub. Some of them looked just plain surprised, others commented on how they appreciated my honesty. But I'm happy that the buyer knew what she was taking on. It's been several years now, and we haven't heard any complaints."

Must You Tell Buyers If Your House Is Haunted?

A few prospective buyers might love the idea of buying a haunted house, but most don't put spectral activity high on their list of must-haves. You're not likely to see a "haunted" box on your state's disclosure form, of course. Nevertheless, you should alert buyers to odd or unexplained activity—rooms that won't warm up, noises that sound like dancing in your attic at night, and so on—regardless of what you believe to be the basis.

Home buyers have actually sued over undisclosed hauntings. For example, when Jeffrey Stambovsky bought a turreted turn-of-the-century Victorian in Nyack, New York, in 1990, he wasn't familiar with local legends. Nor had the seller disclosed her experiences to him, which included a ghost that periodically shook her daughter's bed, another that hovered in midair, and one that dressed as a Navy lieutenant during the American Revolution and confronted her son "eyeball to eyeball outside the basement door."

Once Stambovsky got wind of all this, he wanted out of the purchase. He got his way, but only after taking the seller and real estate agent to court, claiming fraudulent misrepresentation. Eventually, a New York appellate court made the astonishing ruling that the house was haunted as a matter of law, because the former owner had previously reported the ghosts to the media. (See *Stambovsky v. Ackley*, 169 A.D.2d 254 (N.Y. App. Div. 1991).)

The one caveat to the above "disclose everything" advice is if your state's laws specifically say that you don't need to give out a certain type of information. Such provisions are most often included to protect the privacy of previous homeowners. In New York, for example, home sellers and their brokers are legally exempt from disclosing that a previous owner or occupant of the property had, or was suspected of having, HIV, AIDS, or any other unspecified disease that's unlikely to be easily transmittable through occupancy of a dwelling place. (See N.Y. Real Prop. Law § 443a-1.) In practical terms, that means that you shouldn't enter such information on the disclosure form; but neither should you (or your agent) lie about it if asked directly. The best way to deal with such a provision is to decline to answer the relevant question.

> **TIP**
>
> **Don't fill out your disclosure form in one sitting.** You probably won't remember every little issue during your first pass at the form. The next day, you may wake up thinking, "Wait a minute, didn't we put duct tape over that hole in the … ." It's best not to turn the form over to your real estate agent or buyers until you're sure you've really finished.

Your Real Estate Agent's Obligation to Disclose Home-Related Information

In some, but not all states, a home's listing agents must tell buyers about any conditions they notice on the property that the seller didn't mention in the disclosures. This serves as a check on a seller's instincts to hide problems with the home, and reinforces the agent's professional and ethical obligation to deal fairly with buyers.

Agents in your state might either have a standard form of their own to fill out, or they may be asked to fill in a small section of your disclosure form. Even in states that don't require agents to affirmatively offer up information to buyers, outright fraud in communicating with buyers or answering their questions is a legal no-no.

Like you, the listing agent will not be required to conduct an in-depth inspection of the property; at least, not beyond what can be viewed in the course of preparing it for sale. Also like you, the listing agent is required to list only "material" or important defects that would affect the home's value or desirability.

Nevertheless, during the course of the transaction a seasoned listing agent who has gone through numerous home sales may pick up facts about your home that you'd missed. Perhaps the agent notices a strange slope in the floor during a walk-through—something you didn't disclose because you'd gotten so accustomed to it that you'd stopped noticing. The agent realizes that this might indicate problems with the foundation and so must let the buyer know about the slope, in writing.

Experienced agents also know that openness about what they observe about a home enhances both their professional reputation and the confidence of the other agents and buyers in the sale. So you may find that your agent mentions a few little items that you might not consider "material," such as a small snag in the carpet.

When and How to Give the Form to Prospective Buyers

By when, exactly, you are expected to give the disclosure form to your prospective buyers depends on law as well as state custom. In a few states, disclosures are made available to anyone considering the purchase. In most, the seller can wait until the buyer is in contract—that is, you have formally accepted the buyer's offer.

Be sure the buyer acknowledges receipt of your disclosures, by signing and dating the form.

CAUTION
Your disclosure obligations don't end after you hand over the form. What if a new issue arises on your property between time you give the disclosure form to the buyer and the closing date? For example, perhaps moisture starts seeping through your roof or basement floor for the first time. Your state's law will likely require you to advise the buyer of the new concern, by either updating or amending your disclosure form.

Legal Liability If You Disobey State Disclosure Laws

If you violate the disclosure law by misrepresenting or failing to disclose required information, whether it was intentional or careless, and the buyer discovers this after moving in, you may be in legal trouble. The buyer may sue you for failure to disclose, fraud, or misrepresentation (intentional or negligent).

A buyer who is successful in such a lawsuit may be awarded substantial monetary damages. In unusual cases, courts may void the contract and return all property or money back to the buyer and to you, as if the purchase had never occurred.

Federal Lead Disclosure Laws

If selling a house built before 1978, you must, no matter where you live in the U.S., comply with a federal law called the Residential Lead-Based Paint Hazard Reduction Act of 1992 (U.S. Code § 4852d), also known as Title X. This requires you to:

- disclose all known lead-based paint and hazards in the house
- give buyers a pamphlet prepared by the U.S. Environmental Protection Agency (EPA) called "Protect Your Family From Lead in Your Home"
- include certain warning language in the contract as well as signed statements from all parties verifying that all requirements were completed
- keep signed acknowledgements for three years as proof of compliance, and
- give buyers a ten-day opportunity to test the house for lead.

If you fail to comply with Title X requirements, the buyer can sue you for triple the amount of damages actually suffered. For more information on lead hazards, prevention, and disclosures, and to download the required pamphlet, get in touch with the National Lead Information Center (800-424-LEAD or www.epa.gov/lead; click "Real Estate Disclosure Information" for the pamphlet).

State Laws on Location of Sex Offenders

Every state in the U.S. has adopted some version of "Megan's Law," which requires state law enforcement authorities to maintain, and make publicly available, information on the home addresses of registered sex offenders. (The law is named after seven-year-old Megan Kanka, a New Jersey girl who was raped and killed by a known registered sex offender who had, unbeknownst to her family, moved into a residence across the street.)

Many states have also added a notice to their disclosure forms alerting buyers to the availability of their state's registered sex offender database. This doesn't mean that you yourself will have to actually look up the presence of sex offenders in your neighborhood and advise the buyers about it—though if you know of a neighbor who presents an active threat with regard to this or any other sort of crime, you probably do need to disclose this. Your state form will more likely include boilerplate language advising buyers that they can look up this information on their own. ●

Spiffing Up Your House:
Decluttering, Cleaning, and Staging

Making your house look its best for open houses and other showings is a crucial part of the marketing process. This is true whether the real estate market is hot, cold, or middling. As houses get easier to sell, however, it may be tempting to skip some of the recommended steps—to simply open your doors and say, "Here it is!" even if you're still living in the house with all your stuff, or have moved out and left empty, cavernous rooms behind.

Is doing the minimum a sensible approach? That's ultimately a strategic decision, to be made with the help of your real estate agent. But if you've got the time, energy, and resources, spending some of them polishing your house's look can produce instant and significant rewards. In a down market, it might help produce that one crucial offer. In a hot one, it might produce a slew of competing, and therefore high-priced, offers.

The most important thing to remember as you decide how much to do is that buyers' imaginations are not as vivid as you might expect. They can't always peer through clutter to see the potential that lies beneath; nor see past mementos to visualize the house as their own; nor mentally fill an empty room with their own possessions.

Your goal in preparing your house for showings is to do that job for them—in fact, to make your house look so fantastic that they start dreaming of a new, more beautiful life for themselves. Even in a development where all the homes were built around the same time, with similar designs, a staged home can look fresher, larger, and better maintained than the unstaged one for sale down the block.

This chapter will acquaint you with the established real estate industry principles regarding what makes a house show well. Then you can implement whatever level of changes you decide are appropriate, perhaps including:

- decluttering, depersonalizing, and cleaning
- decorating on your own or with the help of your real estate agent (if he or she has these skills), and/or
- hiring a professional stager.

First, the Basics: Declutter, Depersonalize, and Clean

Roll up your sleeves. Stuffing all your extra junk into a basement or closet may work when the in-laws visit, but buyers are likely to open every single door and poke around. A stuffed-full closet will make them think, "Not enough storage." In any event, few houses have enough storage space to fit all the stuff you'll need to remove from living spaces before buyers start tromping around.

Many real estate experts advise that you start by simply getting rid of half of your possessions. Yes, that's 50%. Whether you toss, sell, move into storage, or take the stuff with you to your next home, the place will likely sell much better once its insides have been pared down to what's either essential or beautiful.

You'll likely find that it's hard to make decisions about permanently disposing of possessions without the involvement of other people in your household. Try to get everyone in the same room, to discuss what stays and what goes.

Declutter

Decluttering sounds easy in theory: Most people understand that their mantelpiece may have more knickknacks than it really needs, or that their antique stuffed animal collection isn't universally appealing. But decluttering is much more than that. Here are some specific guidelines:

- **If it's just to look at, it's probably not necessary.** Artworks and decorative objects are not always clutter. A simple print can enhance a blank wall, for example. But you should look at each item and decide whether it adds aesthetic value and fits the overall look that you'd like your house to have. If not, pack it up and enjoy it in your new home.
- **Bookcases should not be full of books!** Shelf space often looks better with a select few books, in combination with attractive bookends, plus a few vases and other decorative items.

- **If you haven't used it in six months, pack it up.** That immersion blender you bought at a garage sale and never used? The unopened racetrack Grandma gave your 17-year old for his birthday? Put those away for now, or sell or donate them.

- **You probably need less than half the clothes in your closet.** Box up seasonal items and those you rarely wear, shoes included. When in doubt, try your clothes on. For most people, this eliminates a goodly portion of what's in the closet. Make sure what's remaining looks neat and well organized—all nicely folded, hung, or arranged.

- **Countertops, desks, and tables must be clear.** This can be tough when you're still living in a house during showings. You'll need to deal with not only newspapers and magazines, but also bills and letters, and all those other stacks of paper that tend to pile up. A rule that the pros follow: Have only one visible object for every eight square feet of flat surface (especially in marketing photos).

- **Remove a third of your furniture.** Start with the obvious: bookcases (books can easily be stored), footstools or ottomans that are convenient but take up space, and a china cabinet in an already overcrowded dining room. In the short term, you'll hardly miss them.

- **Your kitchen could stand to lose a few.** Whether you're a gourmet chef or an expert at the art of microwaving, you're probably not regularly using many of the utensils, appliances, and other items in your kitchen. We'll talk more about kitchen staging below.

- **Pretend you're living in a vacation rental.** If you've ever rented a cabin, it probably came with the bare minimum: one corkscrew, one frying pan, one set of towels. Its sparseness may have been inconvenient, but you made do. Emulate that to make your house—including cupboards, closets, and storage spaces—feel larger.

- **Organize everything that's staying behind.** For example, papers and receipts can be stored in patterned or colored boxes that match your décor.

> **TIP**
> **You may need a storage space for the overflow.** First, try bartering for space with family or friends, with the promise that you'll pick everything up as soon as you move. Another option is transportable storage units (big containers you can park outside), often called "pods."

Depersonalize

The fewer clues you leave that a specific person lives in your home, the easier it will be for a buyer to imagine living there. Depersonalizing isn't just about removing literal images of you and your family, however. To erase your own influence, you should:

- **Hide all friends' photos and cards.** Remove photos on the wall or, in bare spots, replace them with simple prints (images of attractive but forgettable locations, flowers, and so forth). Also get rid of friends' and relatives' Christmas photos, postcards, or baby announcements on the refrigerator or mantle.

- **Eliminate pet smells, hair, and more.** It's hard to neutralize the effect of pets in your home, but do your best. Make sure there's no dog bowl in the kitchen or kitty litter box in the bathroom, and if possible, get your pets out of the home for every showing. (That means out of the yard, too. Your dog's barking may be meant as, "Hello!," but buyers may hear it as, "Go away or I'll take a piece out of your leg!") If your pets will be there during times when agents bring buyers for individual showings, contain them as best you can, and make sure your listing mentions their presence, along with the pet's name, so the agent or prospective buyers don't startle the animal.

> **TIP**
> **Ask friends for honest opinions.** Being objective about your own space can be difficult, so ask friends with good taste to point out things you might overlook. Start with, "If you were thinking of buying this house, what would top the list of things you don't like or seem too personal?" Assure them that your feelings won't be hurt. You might even hold a mini "open house" for neighbors or friends to share these perspectives and give feedback.

- **Get rid of any strong odors.** When you first step into your house after being away for several hours, put it through the sniff test. Find and eliminate any sources of odors, even if it's only garlic or curry. You may want to use scented candles or neutralizing sprays in the kitchen and bathroom, too. (But don't go overboard spraying chemical products, or you'll turn off some buyers.) If you're a smoker, start stepping outside to light up, store the ashtray out of sight, and throw away butts.

- **Remove distinct artwork, décor, and collections.** A collection of spoons, antique irons, or ethnic masks is a statement about you and what you value or spend your time doing. Such personal statements detract from selling your house.

- **Neutralize color.** If you thought a red dining room would be a fun statement, or let your daughter paint her room deep purple, you may need to repaint. Go for warm but neutral shades. ("There's a reason they call it 'realtor beige,'" says Realtor Amy Robeson. "Your color choices need to appeal to the broadest possible market.") Also remove or replace any clashing accent pillows, towels, curtains, or other accessories.

- **Put away signs of religion, politics, or ideology.** Your beliefs (or those of your children) may speak well of you, but they are also highly personal, and close another door to buyers thinking of the house as potentially theirs. Besides, there's no sense alienating prospective buyers whose views differ from yours. Similarly, if you have any paraphernalia that speaks to a potentially polarizing view—the legalization of marijuana, for example—stash it away for now.

Even after you've taken those steps, look around one last time for stray personal items. A child's team trophy? Put it away.

Clean, Clean, and Clean

When you show your home, it must be spotless. This not only makes the space look its best, it suggests that you take good care of it. You may already keep things pretty clean. But lots of the dirt in your home may be invisible, or will emerge only after you start decluttering: the dust that accumulates on the top of ceiling fans, the gunk that's growing in the back of the cabinet under the sink, the grime that builds up on the windowsills. Get rid of it. Also polish any hardware, such as brass faucets and doorknobs.

If you're not feeling up to the task, hire someone else to do an initial deep clean. This may cost you a couple hundred dollars, but will ensure that things are in great shape to start. Other good tasks to leave to professionals include steaming carpets, washing all the windows (inside and out), and power washing cement stairs and porches.

Dress-Up Time! How Staging Works

"Staging" homes for sale has taken the real estate industry by storm in the last decade or two. If you bought your house before that, your first instinct may be to roll your eyes—but keep reading, particularly if staging has become a common practice in the area where you live.

Staging basically means using design, décor, and lighting to make your house's most attractive features apparent while minimizing its less-than-perfect aspects. Luckily, getting prospective buyers focused on the right things doesn't mean having to remodel your house. Once you understand the principles at work, you can implement many of them yourself or decide to turn them over to others.

Does Staging Really Make a Difference to Buyers?

Any number of real estate agents will tell you that staging works. Not too surprisingly, so will the stagers themselves. But objective studies do seem to back up their assertions, with findings that staging leads to either higher home prices or fewer days on the market before the house is sold.

For example, a HomeGain survey (2012) found that putting $724 into staging a house yielded a $2,145 increase in the sales price. And the Real Estate Staging Association (RESA®) conducted a 2013 study that compared the number of days on the market between staged and unstaged houses (both vacant and occupied). The staged houses sold 87% faster—after 40 days on the market, as opposed to 143 days for the unstaged homes.

Even a highly publicized contrary survey conducted in 2014 ("The Impact of Staging Conditions on Residential Real Estate Demand"), which found that buyers who viewed online images of staged homes were savvy enough to not assign higher values to the staged ones, found that the study subjects thought *other* home buyers would spend more on staged homes. That's a crucial consideration in any multiple-bidding situation.

Yet it can be hard for sellers to see why staging is worth the cost or effort. Your house may be perfectly nice looking and comfortable. The key thing to remember about staging, however, is that it's not about living in your home, it's about selling it.

Making the house appealing to as many people as possible may mean seeing—and changing—unusual or unattractive features that aren't even on your radar. There's a bit of theater involved. You're making your house look its best, so that everyone who comes in imagines living the wonderful life suggested by the stylish yet comfy décor, and hopefully, wants to buy in.

> **TIP**
>
> **When is staging a home not worth it?** "If the place is clearly a fixer, staging it may not make sense," says California Realtor Ira Serkes. "I recommend just tidying it up—cleaning the house, washing the windows, and perhaps painting. But in most cases, sellers definitely benefit from editing their possessions at the very least. I'd say around 80% of my sellers stage their homes."

Steps to a Successful Staging

A worthwhile staging effort usually involves:
- repainting
- removing all but a select few pieces of furniture and other décor
- replacing existing furniture with a few well-chosen (and sometimes smaller) pieces

- creating themes and unity for the various rooms (making a home office look like a child's bedroom, perhaps, or turning a space between the kitchen and garage into an attractive, functional office)
- using decorative and lighting techniques to draw the eye away from unappealing aspects of the house, and
- adding finishing touches such as flowers, cushions, and bowls of fruit.

It's all both easier and harder than it sounds. And, of course, you want to avoid that artificial, fake look that a badly staged home projects.

> **CAUTION**
>
> **Your excellent taste may be different from most buyers' taste.** While some buyers may love unique features like an elaborate, antique Queen Anne dining table and rose-patterned wallpaper, or an ultra-modern treatment in black, white, and chrome, most won't. If your house has a particular architectural style, you might emphasize this feature with furniture and accessories that complement it. But don't go overboard—you don't want people with different aesthetics to think their possessions won't work in the space.

Timing Your Staging

If you plan to stage your home, it's best to do so before opening the place to photographers or buyers. You may feel like you're losing valuable time keeping your house off the market while you stage it, but you will likely be able to recoup some of that "lost time" when it sells quickly.

Also, you'll get the most interest and attention from agents and buyers during your home's first ten days on the market. If you don't stage from the start, and don't receive the quantity or quality of offers you were anticipating, that first rush of buyers isn't going to come back. Although new prospects may come in after them, they won't arrive at the same rate. You'll have lost valuable time and the chance to make a real splash with your home's entry onto the market.

Still Living in the House? Coping With the Staging

If it's possible to move out of your house before putting it on the market, that will offer many advantages. Your toothbrushes and kitty litter box will magically disappear from the scene!

Unfortunately, moving out simply isn't possible for many home sellers. If that's the case for you, you're going to have to live without a lot of your life's conveniences. And you may have to spend an unusual amount of time on everyday tasks—pulling your toaster or coffee maker out from a cabinet in order to use it, then putting it back when you're done, for instance.

Also, you'll soon learn that there's an art to arranging pillows or tossing a blanket in that casually elegant way. Some people have it, others may, if they hired a professional stager, have to call and say, "Help! Please redo this!"

Just remember, it's all temporary. And it's precisely because your current home setup is so inconvenient—with no relation to everyday living—that it seems so appealing. Look at all that kitchen counter space with the toaster gone!

Moved On? Staging a Vacant House

When we said it's best to move, we didn't necessarily mean taking all your furniture with you. Vacant houses don't sell well. They feel cold and forbidding and are easily forgotten. Buyers have trouble imagining how a vacant house will look after it's furnished or even how big it really is. They may instead obsess over easily viewed blemishes, like scratches in the floorboards or scuff marks on the baseboards.

Worse for your bottom line, the emptiness may telegraph to buyers that you're already paying for a new place and eager to unload this one—perhaps at a lower price.

A vacant house does, however, give you an opportunity to dress the place up without having to conceal your existence there. You can choose pieces of your own furniture and decorative items (if you can spare them or haven't already moved them across the country) to make the house look like a home. If you hire a professional stager, that person may bring in pieces of furniture, or confer with you over which items of yours to use.

"I basically moved twice," observes Carter, after having sold her house in Boston. "The first time was after packing up after the decluttering, and moving my personal items to my next home. I left behind furniture and accessories, so that the place would show well. Then after the sale, it was time to pack up for the second move."

*L*esson learned the hard way **Should have staged my empty house from day one.** When Kyung sold her house in Pennsylvania, she says, "My Realtor told me to basically strip the place bare. So I followed her advice. My son repainted and hung new wallpaper. Then we waited for offers—and none came in at all. Finally, we got a stager to come put fake stuff in the empty home. It sold a few weeks later."

Should You Hire a Professional Stager?

Home staging is a career with its own cadre of professionals and related resources. The most highly trained receive a designation such as Certified Staging Professional™, but others (including some real estate agents), may have staging skills.

Experienced stagers have done what you're seeking to do many times before. Their experience will tell them what buyers react positively to. They can come into your space, figure out its problems, and maximize its benefits. And because they're used to specializing in one geographical area, they'll be familiar with local tastes and preferences.

Staging professionals aren't cheap. Their fees can easily reach several thousand dollars, depending on the size of your home, how much of your own furniture the stager uses, and how much work the place needs. But stagers will also work with your budget, and typically offer different levels of service.

Consult only. For starters, the stager may be willing to do a one-off consultation and provide a report for a relatively small fee—around $250 to $350. This report (which is usually the first step when hiring a stager in any case) will tell you what needs to be done, room by room. You'd then decide which of these recommendations to implement yourself.

Something in between. As a middle-ground option, you can hire the stager to make the place look nice with mostly existing materials. This means you won't plan to do major work or bring in a lot of new furniture and decorative items. The stager may simply suggest what stays and what goes, rearrange furniture, and coach you on what further things you might do. Of course, this approach tends to work best on homes that already look good and happen to match prevailing tastes.

The whole enchilada. If you choose the right professional for the job, going all out with a full staging can be an efficient use of money. The stager will come up with a plan, bring in furniture and decorative items, and even serve as a project manager for making repairs and small improvements. The stager may, for example, hire an electrician to replace a dated light fixture or hire a carpenter to repair or replace a door. Because the stager will have many contacts, you'll be spared the hassle of finding high-quality professionals or negotiating with them. (And if the various contractors' fees are coming out of the stager's fee, remember that it's not really fair to call it an "expensive" staging. You would have had to pay the electrician or carpenter in any case.)

How much will all this cost, exactly? Experts advise spending roughly 1% to 1.5% of your home's selling price on a full-scale staging. Some stagers charge flat fees for certain services, others may charge on an hourly basis, especially for tasks like project management.

> ## CAUTION
> **Will your agent pay for the stager?** A rare few agents will do so, but most regard it as just another service, like painting, that the homeowner should cover. Besides, hiring your own stager gives you more control over the process.

Choosing a Stager

If you've decided that staging would be a good investment, choose a stager whose work you have seen and genuinely like. Particularly if you're living in the home, you don't want to be annoyed rather than impressed by the changes. In many cases, real estate professionals will recommend stagers they've worked with in the past. But you can also get names from friends and neighbors who've sold homes, and visit local open houses and ask who did the staging.

> **CAUTION**
> **The cheapest stager isn't necessarily the one to choose.** If a stager's price is a lot lower than others it may be because the stager uses cheap materials (for example, inexpensive furniture), which won't do as much to sell your home.

Once you have a few leads, do a little homework. Start by looking at the stager's website. They typically post before-and-after pictures of homes they've staged. The website should also indicate the type of experience the stager has gained, and any training or certifications. (The website for the Real Estate Staging Association, www.realestatestagingassociation.com, explains some of the available programs.)

> *L*esson learned the hard way **Next time, we'll make sure we actually like the stager!** Sybil and George had already bought their next home, and with two small children, were feeling the time pressure of preparing their first house for sale. They went with the agent's suggestion for a particular home stager. But, Sybil says, "We were then horrified at having to spend money for only slightly varying shades of brown paint on the walls, décor that seemed tacky within our traditional Arts and Crafts bungalow home, and over-the-top touches like champagne glasses on the bedspread. The sale was successful, with more than one offer—but the new owner thought the champagne glasses were ridiculous too, and promptly repainted the brown walls."

The next step is to contact stagers you're potentially interested in. You may set up an appointment right away, or get some of your questions answered over the phone. Ask about experience, cost, and availability at the time you plan to sell. A professional stager won't be able to give you a quote without seeing your home, but should be able to give you a ballpark figure, based on your accurate description of the property.

You can also ask for references of satisfied clients and to see additional photos. Finally, make sure the stager has proper insurance—he or she will be in your home, and you want to know you're protected if someone is injured in the process of staging it, or that damage to the home or property (intentional or otherwise) will be covered.

Alternatives to Hiring a Professional Stager

If the expense of hiring a professional stager seems prohibitive, you might explore alternatives. For example, if you know your house needs to be organized or freed from junk, there's a whole industry dedicated to helping you with just that task. The organizers of the world can give you tips on evaluating, tossing, and sorting everything into neat files and boxes. (Think how much easier your move will be!)

To find an organizer near you, visit the National Association of Professional Organizers® (www.napo.net). Look for someone with experience in home organizing (versus office or business organizing).

For aesthetic tips, you might buy a few hours of a designer's time. Ask for general tips about what you can do to make the place look better, and expect answers like, "That corner needs a lamp that directs light toward the ceiling," or "This color is too loud for a small bathroom." You can then implement these changes yourself.

As we've mentioned, some real estate agents also offer staging skills. We recommend you choose an agent primarily based on real estate expertise and ability to sell your home (discussed in Chapter 2), without expecting too much in the staging department. Nevertheless, your agent spends a lot of time looking at houses, and if he or she is aesthetically inclined to boot, why not take advantage of the agent's recommendations?

> ⭐ **B**est thing we ever did **Didn't follow all of our agent's staging recommendations.** When Doug put his home on the market, his real estate agent had lots of suggestions for sprucing up the house. "However," said Doug, "it soon became clear that our agent was a wannabe home designer. Some of her suggestions were great, like replacing a ratty-looking door and repainting the front porch But some were crazy given the hot sellers' market we were in, like repainting the entire interior of the home in designer colors even though the existing neutral-colored paint was fresh or replacing the almost brand-new kitchen floor tile with wood. The house got multiple offers over our asking price, and the buyers ended up remodeling the whole kitchen anyway. We saved quite a bit of money by following our own instincts."

If you're strapped for cash or simply like the idea of a do-it-yourself (DIY) project, you can do your own staging job. We'll give you advice below on how to pull it off, and many books are available on the subject.

DIY Staging Outside: Maximizing Curb Appeal

If you decide to stage your home yourself, the place to start is outside. The front of your home is the first thing prospective buyers see, and some won't bother to get out of their car if their first impression is negative. Here are tips for making your home exterior look good from the front:

- **Pack up what's going with you.** Pick up any toys, gardening equipment, and debris. If you have a porch, sweep it and clean off any furniture. Get rid of clutter—bye-bye garden gnomes and flamingos.
- **Spruce up the garden.** Mow the lawn, pull up weeds, and trim the hedges. Replace any plants that didn't survive the last

storm or drought, and trim off dead portions of living plants. If you don't have time to do this yourself, pay someone else to do it (and depending on timing, to maintain it). Make sure you're giving plants enough water, on a regular schedule.

- **Add new plants.** Some new, blooming foliage might brighten things up. Potted plants on either side of the front door add a cheerful touch and are easy to care for. (If the plants die, you can quickly replace them.) Plus, unless the planters are so big as to be considered "fixtures," you can take them with you when you move.

- **Lay out a new welcome mat.** This small and inexpensive gesture will make a good impression and help keep your floors clean. You can take the mat with you, too.

- **Add a small table and chairs.** No one ever seems to actually dine in their front yard. Nevertheless, creating a scene that implies you've had many leisurely brunches there suggests to buyers that they'll also be enjoying the good life.

- **Touch up or repaint.** If your house is truly in need of an exterior paint job, this can be money well spent. But if the paint just has a few trouble spots—peeling around the windows, for example— just do a simple touch-up. Also consider painting the door and window trim; these small accents will have a big impact.

- **Wash windows and siding.** Cleaning the windows will make a big difference both inside and out, freshening the appearance of your home and letting in more natural light. Wash screens or take them down (store them in the garage). Also make sure the driveway and sidewalk are clean (a pressure washer works well), as well as the external siding.

- **Get rid of cobwebs or signs of pests.** Spider webs, for example in the corners of your porch ceiling and around windows, make a house look unkempt. Spray for spiders if you have problems; this will prevent them from reappearing.

- **Clear downspouts and gutters.** Even if it's the middle of summer, clean gutters look neater and show that you take good care of your home.

- **Make sure the house is well lit.** First off, buyers need to be able to see your house number. Make sure it's clearly visible, and repaint or replace it if necessary. Then step outside and check whether all the other lovely features of your home can be clearly seen at any time of day or night. Many buyers drive by at night. (It's also a good idea to have an attractive evening shot on your website.) Consider putting outdoor lights on a timer that goes on automatically, or buy inexpensive solar lights for a walkway or landscaping.
- **Get rid of old cars.** Buyers are put off by clunkers in the driveway.

The back yard won't control the buyer's first impression, but it's arguably just as important. That's because it's a functional space—buyers will look forward to treating it like another room, especially in warmer climates. Do the same kind of cleanup you did in the front.

If the backyard space doesn't already appear to be useful (other than for staring at from a window), take steps to make it so. If you don't have a back deck or patio area, consider whether you can either build one (it's a project that offers a high return on investment) or alter the space to create that illusion. For instance, you might place a patio table on the lawn and surround it with lights and potted plants. Get budget ideas for a simple patio on do-it-yourself websites like www.hgtv.com or www.diynetwork.com.

DIY Staging Inside: Room by Room

Though each room must be cleaned, depersonalized, and decluttered, different rooms call for specific treatment. Here are some easy, inexpensive (or even free!) ways to make each room look its best. After you're done implementing these tips, take a last look at each room to see whether it has a cohesive look.

Then add finishing touches—for example, by setting the dining room table to look like a dinner party is about to happen. This can help create a positive focal point, drawing buyers' eyes to the room's best features. (Just don't overdo it—more than one faux party at a time strains visitors' credulity.)

RESOURCE

Get ideas from photos of professional stagers' work. Many stagers' websites include pictures, which are great for seeing how an uninspiring space can be transformed. Search for "home stager" or check the websites of stagers recommended by your friends and real estate agent. A simple Internet search for "how to stage your house" will also turn up helpful articles and illustrative photos on popular sites like HGTV.com and Bankrate.com.

No matter which room you're working on, make it light and bright. If your house looks lighter, it will also look bigger and cleaner. Make sure all blinds and curtains are open or replace them with sheers if the view is toward, say, a neighbor's junk pile. You can also use indirect artificial lighting, such as track lighting or lamps that point upward. Make sure the wattage on your lightbulbs is high enough—a mere 20-watt bulb in the bathroom, for example, will make it look dark and dreary.

TIP

Swap out fixtures you want to take with you. The buyer has a right to keep all fixtures, or items permanently attached or affixed to the property, such as chandeliers and other lights, outdoor plants, and built-in appliances. But it's still your house, and there's no law against replacing fixtures before the buyer ever sees them. If you know that you'll want to use your trusty stove in your new home, trade it out now—before the buyer has a chance to assume it comes with the house. Of course, your replacements should be attractive and preferably new, even if you pay less for them than you did for the original fixtures.

Kitchen

The kitchen is one of the home's most important rooms, and one that buyers will take a close look at. Here are some tips for making yours look great:

- **Hide the appliances.** The turkey roaster and fondue set can probably be boxed up for now, along with any other appliances you use only occasionally. Put the equipment you'll need regularly under the counter. The same goes for dish soap, sponges, and the rest of what's on your counters.

- **Pack away dishes, utensils, or other items you use only once in a while.** The entire contents of that "catch all" drawer can probably be removed. Also get rid of extras—six wineglasses instead of 12 should hold you for the next few months, for example.

- **If you have tile, clean the grout.** Over time, it gets stained. A solution of bleach and water should restore its color.

- **Clean the oven**. It's no one's favorite job, but buyers will look in there.

- **Wipe down and treat the front of cupboards.** Get rid of the inevitable built-up grease and dirt. If you have wood cupboards, use lemon or orange oil to restore their sheen.

- **Hide the garbage can.** This will make the place look cleaner. If you can actually store it in the garage, that will help reduce smells. And speaking of the under-the-sink area, remove all nonnecessary items from this space.

- **Clean out the fridge.** Reduce the number of condiments and get rid of anything moldy. Wipe down the shelves.

- **Clean out cupboards.** Most of your canned and boxed food items can probably be boxed up for the move. Or, challenge yourself to start working your way through them before the house is listed. Wipe down these shelves, as well, or change the shelf liners.

- **Wipe down walls.** Over time, they get grimy, especially the spot over the stove. The range hood may need a good grease cutter, too—vinegar works well. Ceiling or vent fans may also need special treatment.

- **Get rid of kitchen kitsch.** If you have knickknacks or a cute decorating theme—country old-fashioned, for example—it's time to downplay it. The kitchen should be a fairly neutral room, with the clean, welcoming look of a place where anyone would like to prepare a meal.

- **Fill a bowl with fruit.** Nothing looks homier than food. A filled-up, glass cookie jar or a fresh-baked pie are also warm touches for open houses.

Bathroom

The bathroom is another place to which buyers pay particular attention. It should feel clean, spacious, and ideally, reminiscent of a spa. Here are a few ways to make that happen.

- **Buy new, matching towels in a neutral color.** Even if you currently have neutral-colored towels, new ones will look luxurious and inviting. Don't use these towels. Keep the ones you're actually using out of sight, perhaps temporarily stored in your dryer.
- **Change the shower curtain.** Especially in a small bathroom, a light-hued, solid color, fabric shower curtain makes the space feel large and luxurious.
- **Add a few decorative accessories.** The bathroom counter is a bad place to store personal hygiene products, but a great place for a vase of fresh flowers or a pretty candleholder. You can also use these small decorative items to add color to complement the neutral tones in the room.
- **Clean the vent fan.** It tends to accumulate dirt over time and may be something you rarely notice since it's not in your direct line of sight.
- **Check for mold or mildew in the shower.** This is an automatic and loud turnoff; it suggests there may be more mold lurking elsewhere. Bleach and water should do the trick. Also check the ceiling, especially over the shower.
- **Store all toiletries in a cupboard.** Keep the countertops clear.
- **Clean out the medicine cabinet.** Get rid of old prescriptions that you don't use. (While you're at it, hide the rest of your prescriptions: Open-house visitors have been known to steal painkillers and other widely used medications.)
- **Keep it simple in the shower.** You really need only one bottle of shampoo and conditioner and a bar or bottle of soap. Store these under the sink to give the shower a fresh look.
- **Set out a dispenser of liquid hand soap.** This is less messy than bar soap. Spring for a luxury brand with a pleasant scent such as lavender.

- **Clean out the drain.** Drains clog and slow down with a steady, often unnoticeable accumulation of hair and soap residue. An easy, natural way to keep your drain maintained: Pour in a cup of baking soda, a cup of salt, and a cup of vinegar. (Don't premix this, put it right in the drain itself—otherwise you'll have a minivolcano on your hands!) After 15 minutes, follow with some boiling water.

By the way, prospective homebuyers may use your bathroom while touring your house, so be ready to wash or refold the towels, or put in nice paper ones.

Living or Family Room

This is where people envision spending most of their communal time. You can make it look like a pleasant gathering spot using these tips:

- **Get the TV out of sight.** If it can't be moved, at least make sure it's not turned on while a buyer is visiting.
- **Clear a pathway through the room.** Arrange furniture so that it's comfortable not only to sit and talk in, but to walk around.
- **Brighten up dead zones, most likely in corners.** If a corner is unoccupied, consider putting a floor lamp there. Or buy large potted plants that will make the corner look naturally lush and inviting.
- **Keep it simple.** Make sure the room hasn't become a multipurpose pool table, art projects, and bike storage room.
- **Get rid of oversized furniture.** Remove bulkier pieces like an oversized sofa or armchair; they make the room look smaller. If your sofa is the only place to sit in the room, at least get rid of accents that make it look extra imposing, like throw pillows or blankets.
- **Choose a color scheme, and stick with it.** If you have a yellow couch that clashes with your green chairs, offset by a purple rug, you'll confuse and overstimulate buyers' senses. Either cover or remove furniture or accessories that don't match. A slipcover can be an inexpensive yet effective option for updating an old couch, too.

- **Decorate the walls.** You don't want walls that are totally bare. While it's a good idea to take down your family photos, don't leave huge blank spots, especially if you can see lines where they've been hung. Choose two or three tasteful photographs or prints, in frames, to deal with the barest walls.
- **Dress up the fireplace.** A fireplace, if you have one, can make a great focal point to your living room. But if the screen has gotten dusty or torn, hide it (or at least wash and repaint it). Many stagers replace the screen with an eye-catching new one. Also scrub the bricks or tiles, sweep out ashes, and put fresh logs on the fire.

> **TIP**
> **Don't have the right furniture? You can rent it.** Try rental companies near you, or visit Cort Furniture (www.cort.com). If a friend or family member has the right item, you may even be able to borrow it—or exchange it, perhaps for a nice meal out or a few nights of free babysitting.

Bedrooms

Bedrooms are more than just places to sleep. They're havens in which each member of a family hopes to relax and enjoy personal space. Here are ways to make the bedrooms especially appealing to buyers.

- **Don't hide clutter under the bed.** If buyers look there, they'll instantly be wise to your scheme (though you might get away with this by using nice-looking under-bed storage pieces).
- **Buy new linens.** You can inexpensively brighten and freshen the space by putting a new cover on the bed and adding a couple of attractive and well-coordinated pillows. Make sure the bed cover matches nicely with everything else in the room, like curtains, rug, and walls.
- **Stick to basic furniture.** You don't need much more than a bed, side tables, and a dresser. If those items are big and bulky, consider removing or replacing them.

- **Make sure your room looks like a getaway from regular life.** In particular, remove the desk or television.
- **Gender-neutralize children's rooms.** A pink canopied bed or one in the shape of a race car screams girl or boy; it will be harder for someone with a child of the opposite gender—or no child at all—to see beyond this.
- **Get rid of large toys.** Plastic kids' toys in loud colors are particularly unattractive. Have kids choose a handful of their favorite toys, then pack the rest away for the next house.

> **TIP**
>
> **Get the kids involved.** Talk to them about the temporary changes and regular cleanups that are part of selling your home. Think about incentives: Whether it's a new toy in return for packing away less-frequently used ones or a special privilege for pitching in to clean the bathroom every day, you may find the process easier if your kids are committed to it.

- **Make sure teenagers keep their rooms clean.** Also take down the ubiquitous posters—bands, heartthrobs, or whatever. Your teens can always reintroduce these in the next house (if their loyalties or obsessions haven't already changed).
- **Don't use bedrooms as lifestyle rooms.** You may have turned an extra bedroom into a craft room, football paraphernalia room, or children's playroom, but most buyers won't be interested in those uses. If you have lots of bedrooms, you might increase buyer interest by converting one to an office. Otherwise, make sure bedrooms are set up to accommodate as many people as are likely to be in your typical buyer's family.
- **Put the hamper in the closet.** This goes for the diaper pail too; and make sure it's a smell-proof one.
- **Keep bedside tables clear.** Get rid of the usual clutter—reading glasses, glass of water, or bottle of hand lotion, for example.
- **Straighten out the closets.** After clearing out all the "extras," make sure all the hangers are facing the same way, your shoes are neatly paired, and everything on shelves is carefully stacked.

TIP

Don't stop there! Every room in your house deserves at least some attention in the staging process. Clean out your basement, attic, and garage. Neatly stack any boxes near—but not against—the wall. (You need to leave space for home inspectors' examinations.) If your basement is dark and gloomy, consider painting the walls and ceiling a light color. Vacuum the garage floor and rafters.

Basements and Storage Areas

Prospective buyers are universally interested in storage space. A space full of boxes and junk just doesn't look as large as it might otherwise. You don't have to go all out and add flowers to the basement and similar areas; just make sure they're clean and empty.

Ta Da! Finishing Touches Before a Showing

After all your hard work, make sure the house continues to look good when a prospective buyer comes along. Here are some tips for both restoring order and completing the vision of an inviting home. Yes, some of this may require occasional mad frenzies if you get a visitor on short notice—or if your house has a lockbox and buyers' agents may bring them by unannounced.

- **Keep a bottle of all-purpose cleaning spray handy in the kitchen and bathroom.** You can do a quick wipe down at a moment's notice. Baby wipes also work well for this.
- **Use microfiber cloths to combat dust and debris.** These are particularly good for dusting wood surfaces or picking up stray pet hairs from a hardwood or other solid-surface floor.
- **Open curtains and turn on lights.** This helps everything look bright and spacious.
- **Get everything off the counters.** Items have probably found their way back there by now. In the kitchen, put things neatly in the dishwasher; in the bathroom, store them under the sink.

- **Make sure beds are made and no clothes are lying around.** Keep a hamper in the closet, or immediately throw everything into the washing machine (you can run it later).
- **Vacuum.** A regular biweekly schedule will help keep things in good order, but you may need to do a touch-up on those dust bunnies.
- **Empty wastebaskets and garbage.** It looks neater and avoids unattractive smells.
- **Check for spots on the windows.** Wipe down trouble spots, like the sliding glass door where the dog's nose leaves smudge marks. A mixture of vinegar and water works well.
- **Make it smell good.** A neutral and consistent aroma around the house—no strong fruit or flower smells, which some people will not like—creates a comfortable ambience.
- **Turn on gentle music.** Jazz or classical is usually best. Keep the volume low enough to be unobtrusive, but high enough to create a relaxed mood and mask outdoor traffic or other noises.
- **Arrange flowers or fruit.** These don't need to be giant, expensive bouquets. But nothing dresses a house up more effectively than an artful selection of blooms. Even a single rose in a vase looks nice in an entryway or windowsill. Ask your florist for suggestions for long-lasting and not too heavily fragrant flowers. Another favorite method stagers use to bring life to a house is a big bowl full of fresh lemons, limes, or oranges.
- **Set the right temperature.** You don't want buyers to feel too hot in the summer or too cold in the winter, so set the thermostat accordingly—and program it to stay on all day if you're no longer living there. If you have a fireplace, you may want to light a fire if it helps set the mood—for example, on a rainy winter afternoon.
- **Look at which car is parked in front.** If it's your teenager's flashy hot rod or a visiting relative's gnarly old pickup with torn-off fenders, ask the owner to move it to the next block.

TIP

You can leave your alarm system on. If your house will be open for buyers to walk through with their agents (most likely because you've moved to your next home and the door has a "lockbox" on it), your agent can put a warning, and the security code, in the MLS. (That's why it's good that some portions of the MLS are not open to the public!)

Pricing Your House to Sell—and Sell High

For most sellers, the goal is to get top dollar for their home. If home values have been appreciating in your area, then a high price may mean you'll turn a decent profit on the sale. If prices in your area have remained stagnant following the recent downturn, getting a good price will minimize your loss.

Of course, you'll soon be encountering prospective buyers whose objective is likely the opposite of yours: They want to pay as little as possible for a house. Yet, depending on the local real estate market, some may end up stretching beyond their original budget to get the home that they want—or any home at all.

With all these competing goals and considerations in mind, setting your home's list price will require some serious thought and strategizing—enough that we've devoted an entire chapter to it. If you set a price too high, it might prevent potential buyers from even taking a look at the place. When that happens, your home may sit on the market, forcing you to ultimately make major price drops.

CAUTION
The need for your home to sell quickly is especially high if you've already bought a new home. Owning two homes means you'll be doubly burdened with paying for a mortgage, homeowners' insurance, and utility and maintenance expenses or homeowners' association fees. This can get expensive, potentially wiping out any profit you make by holding out for a higher price.

But neither should you set the list price so low that it misrepresents the value of your property, leads to a lot of low offers you'd never really accept, and perhaps even makes buyers wonder, "What's wrong with the place?"

Strategically speaking, the ideal is usually for the seller to set a price at or a little below the home's true market value. With that approach, the number of agents and buyers who come check the place out, even for a quick stop on open-house days, goes up markedly. Potential purchasers act quickly, fearing that if they don't take advantage of the good deal, someone else will. And if there's a flood of interest, a bidding war may ensue, driving the house price upward.

So, how do you hit that "just right" list price? Your real estate agent (assuming you hire one) should do the lion's share of the research and be able to suggest a price that's appropriate for your local market. As Berkeley-based Realtor Daniel Stea says, "People outside the real estate industry might be surprised to learn how much of my job involves simply keeping up on the market—what homes have just sold, what price they were listed at, what features they had, and how much they ultimately sold for. One of the main reasons for all this research is to help my home-selling clients set the most accurate and attractive list price."

Nevertheless, we recommend playing an active role in this process rather than just sitting back and waiting for your agent to give you a number. By developing a good sense of your local market, you'll be ready to confidently agree or disagree with your agent's advice, and later to negotiate with buyers from the best possible position, knowing when to give and when to hold firm. This chapter will help you with this process, covering how to:

- research your local market
- develop a sense of how local homes are priced, and
- set a realistic, strategic list price.

CAUTION

Pricing isn't about your own needs. As San Francisco broker George Devine explains, "Some people set their price based on what I call a 'need basis' rather than a 'market basis'—they look at what they think they need to achieve to pay off their current mortgage and cover their remodeling projects, and then to afford their next house. Unfortunately, that has no relation to what buyers will pay."

Step One: Take Your Local Real Estate Market's Temperature

Your house's marketability (which quickly translates into price) will inevitably be affected by the heat of your local market. If you've read recent real estate headlines, you know that the U.S. is emerging from a period where the real estate market was considered "cold" nationwide (with a few exceptional locations). Although few people wanted to put their homes up for sale (in real estate lingo, inventory was low), even fewer buyers were ready to pay for them, and houses tended to languish on the market for long periods of time. That allowed buyers to make less than full-price offers and negotiate for concessions, knowing that the seller might not get another offer any time soon—or at least not before the costs of maintaining the house forced the seller to drop its price.

But the market has been heating up dramatically in many parts of the U.S., and is red-hot in some areas. In a hot market, there are more prospective home buyers than sellers ready and willing to part with their homes. Well-priced houses in hot markets usually sell quickly, as buyers compete to get their foot in the door, sometimes paying far more than the asking price. Only the true duds or grossly overpriced houses get rejected by this anxious flock of house hunters, so the overall inventory of available homes stays low.

Sellers in a hot market often receive multiple offers and can confidently negotiate deals, knowing that if they don't get what they want, another offer will come along soon. The seller may even benefit from waiting, as prices in hot markets tend to climb.

TIP

Markets can be balanced, too. In balanced markets, there are about an equal number of sellers and buyers. Prices tend to be neither rock bottom nor sky high. A balanced market is usually transitional, though—at some point, it's going to tip toward hot (as more buyers realize it's a good time to buy because prices are reasonable) or cold (when lots of sellers become motivated to put their homes on the market, because there seem to be plenty of interested buyers).

No matter what you're reading about the heat of the U.S. real estate market, it's not nearly as important as what's happening in your local area. National averages hide striking variations in local market temperatures. While sellers in San Francisco enjoy watching bidders throw in an extra million to get their hands on a two-bedroom home, sellers in Detroit may await offers for so long that they seriously consider putting the place on eBay.

Your real estate professional can give you a pretty quick picture of whether your local market is hot or cold. But if you're not at that point yet, talk to friends, read your local papers, and then use the following objective indicators to figure out what's going on locally:

- **Average sales price.** Looking at recent home sales can give you a good idea of how much homes are actually selling for. You're looking in particular for prices of comparable homes, or "comps" in real estate lingo. That means homes of a similar size and quality, sold recently (within three to six months or less, the more recently the better), and within the same locale (ideally no more than six blocks in an urban area, but also stopping at any dividing lines like a large street that changes the neighborhood character). You can do some research on sale prices yourself online, although a real estate professional can provide you with more complete information. If the average sales price in your area is falling, that's an indicator of a cold market.

- **Days on market.** Another key bit of information is the average number of days it takes houses in your area to sell. The longer homes remain unsold, the more likely that the market is cold. This number is very predictive, too—when it starts climbing, it's an early indicator that the market is cooling.

- **Inventory.** The "inventory" is the number of houses on the market compared to the average number of buyers in that market. For example, if 4,000 houses are currently for sale and 1,000 houses sell (on average) each month, there's four months' worth of inventory. The more inventory, the cooler the market is likely to be.

- **Wording of real estate ads.** If you see a lot of "price reduced" entries, the market is likely cold. If you see agents advertising their services with pictures of homes "Just sold, with multiple offers!" it's hot, hot, hot.

RESOURCE

Get market information online. If you don't yet have a real estate agent digging into MLS data for you, a lot of helpful information, including average sale prices and days on the market, is available on websites such as www.trulia.com and www.zillow.com (though their accuracy can be questionable). Also check the website of your state's Realtor association.

Careful Pricing Remains Important Even in Hot Markets

Some areas of the U.S. real estate market are so hot that they've got experts worrying about whether a new bubble is forming. You might think that the bevy of eager buyers would wash out any issues of overpricing, but that's not necessarily the case.

"I'm definitely seeing some unrealistic sellers as the market heats up," says Greg Nino, a RE/MAX Realtor in Texas. "Some get wild with their expectations, and think their home is better than the highest-priced comparable. Yes, we're in a sellers' market, but let's not get carried away. Too high an offer won't pass the lender's required appraisal, anyway."

Step Two: Evaluate How Well-Located and Desirable Your Home Is

Houses come in all shapes, sizes, and conditions. A gorgeous house may attract multiple bids even in a cold market, while a rundown one may be overlooked in a hot one. Without being overly optimistic, you'll want to recognize when your house has the potential to attract lots of attention—or what you can change to turn its heat up.

Begin by considering your immediate neighborhood. Pay particular attention to the factors discussed in the last section: Are your neighborhood statistics better, worse, or about the same as the rest of the surrounding area? For example, if homes in your neighborhood are selling quickly and for their full asking prices, your neighbor-hood may be hot, even if the general market in the area isn't.

Can You Afford to Buy Before You Sell?

It's not uncommon, when you're selling one house and buying another, to find the house you want to purchase before you've sold your current home. In such a situation, you may have to come up with a way to make payments on both mortgages.

You have several options: You can pay both out of pocket, if you can afford to; you can take out a home equity loan or line of credit on your current home (though these are harder to get than they once were); or you can borrow from someone you know or another source, with the promise of quick repayment when you sell.

None of these options are ideal. After all, if it takes longer than you expect to sell your current home, you may have much higher expenses than you can comfortably afford. That's why it's important to do as much advance work as possible to understand the market where you're buying as well as selling, prepare your current home for a speedy sale, and organize yourself for the coming move.

A particular neighborhood tends to be hot for some identifiable reason. It might be located near a sought-after feature, like a beach or favorite street for shops and restaurants, or have the best schools in the region. It may be an older, established neighborhood of historic homes in a sea of new developments. It may simply be known as "the" place to live.

If you know your neighborhood has a feature that makes it more desirable than those surrounding it, factor that into your comp analysis. Look only at comparables in your desirable neighborhood, not the next one over—even if it's only a couple of blocks away.

Now, back to your own house. Does it have exceptional characteristics that will attract buyers? If, for example, you have a modest home in a neighborhood full of luxury mansions and a good school district, it may bring in buyers eager to both break into the market and foster their children's education. But if it's a tiny home with no room for children, it may be a tougher sell (unless it's got great remodel potential).

Step Three: Determine Your Home's Market Value

Now it's time to take a closer look at the exact amount that other houses are selling for in order to judge the relative value of your home, or its "fair market value." That doesn't mean you'll list it at that price—just that you'll set the list price with an eye toward bringing in offers at or above that value.

To compare your house's value to that of others on the market, you'll want to look at:

- **A comparative market analysis.** A "CMA" is a report compiled by a real estate professional that gives you information about houses similar to yours (in size, amenities, and location), which are either on the market, have sold, or were listed but expired (possibly because they were priced too high and no one bought) within a reasonably recent time period (ideally three months when the market is in transition, and no more than six months). These sales can tell you how much homes like yours are actually selling for, how long it's taking for them to sell, and what their sale prices are in relation to their list prices. It's especially important to pay attention to the prices of pending, rather than closed, sales, for the basic reason that they're the most recent. (In a rising market, the appropriate price for the house you want to sell may be even higher than the most recent pending comps—and vice versa.)

TIP
You can get a CMA-type analysis without actually hiring a real estate professional. Some websites, such as www.homegain.com, offer a comparative market analysis for free. These are usually prepared by a

local real estate agent who will contact you and probably try to solicit your business. Alternatively, you can pay a small fee for such a report, generated online. For example, at www.ushomevalue.com, $40 will buy you a one-time "appraisal emulation report," which lists several comparable properties that have sold in your neighborhood. That's a huge step up from what you'll get from online appraisal systems like those on www.zillow.com, which will estimate your home's worth, but aren't always up to date, don't take into account a home's special features and aesthetic appeal (remember, it's done using publicly available information; no human eyeballs have evaluated your home's features), and won't give you immediate access to the comparative information that underlies the estimates.

- **List prices versus sale prices.** This is crucially important, and one of the biggest things that people forget when looking at the real estate market. A list price is how much a home is advertised for. It tells you nothing about what it will sell for. You need to find out the difference between how much people are asking for their homes and how much they're actually getting. This will prevent you from unrealistically valuing your property, for example by thinking, "That house down the street is on sale for $250,000—I should be able to get at least $315,000!" If that house actually sells for $225,000, its list price tells you that the seller was perhaps unrealistic—and it says little about your home's actual value. (But if the nearby home actually sells for $270,000, it might tell you that the seller adopted a strategy of pricing low in order to inspire multiple bids.)

- **A professional appraisal.** When you bought your house, the bank probably required you to get it "appraised"—that is, have a professional view it and put a dollar figure on its market value. But homeowners can pay to get appraisals, too. The appraiser will give you a report that arrives at the value of your property by comparing it to others that have recently sold. Keep in mind, however, that the appraiser won't necessarily have actually seen the comparable properties, while a local real estate agent might have. The good news is that because you don't need as much detailed analysis as a bank does, you can ask for a cheaper version of the report, called a "restricted appraisal." It should cost around $100 to $200.

- **Real estate agents.** Even if you don't plan to hire a real estate agent (we discuss the option of selling the property yourself in Chapter 11), it's a good idea to get a few of their opinions as to how much your house is worth. An agent will usually offer an opinion if there's any apparent possibility of being hired. The benefits are that agents are familiar with the local market and can base their estimates on actually seeing the house. Chances are they toured through the other local houses that recently sold. "Sellers almost always estimate high," says seasoned Massachusetts real estate broker Nancy Atwood. "An agent who really knows the market has seen what there is to see and will set the seller straight, making sure they start out with the right price that will attract buyers." Don't believe every agent you hear, though—a few of the less professional ones operate on the theory that they can convince you to list with them by suggesting an artificially high value (called "buying" the listing).

- **Open houses.** Although it's the least scientific measurement, open houses in your neighborhood, even of the houses that aren't quite comparable to yours, can be informative. Viewing these helps you get a real sense of what drives list prices up and down—and, if you listen to some conversations, how buyers are reacting to the list price. You can also simply ask the agent present at the open house whether he or she expects the place to attract offers at or over the list price.

With some combination of the above sources of information in hand, you should be in a good position to arrive at a likely fair market value for your home—or at least a range. If the numbers you're getting still seem to be all over the map, it's probably time to talk to an agent who has seen the individual properties. For example, the low price on a supposedly comparable property might be explained by the fact that it needed a new foundation, or a particularly high-priced house may actually be located across a school district boundary, in a better district.

At Last, Set the List Price: High, Low, or in Between?

Now that you have a good sense of what your house is worth—and therefore how much it should sell for, if all goes well—you'll have to decide what to do with the information. You have three options. Discuss these carefully with your real estate agent, taking your property's likely appeal and local market conditions into account:

- **Set the asking price below the market value.** As we've mentioned, you likely stand the best chance of generating interest if you set a price that's a little below what other, similar homes are listed for. And a low price is especially appropriate if you need to move quickly or are asking buyers to handle a lot of repairs. Potential buyers will see there's a good deal to be had and hopefully come running. Of course, that could mean you end up selling to one of them for a little less than market value. But the more likely scenario, if you've got more than one interested buyer, is that competition between them drives the value back up—perhaps even over the list price. The trick here is not to go too low, which can lead to a frenzy of multiple offers—some that are unrealistically low, and others that are so high that the appraiser won't sign off on the buyer's loan. Seeing the frenzy developing, some prospective buyers may actually back off, afraid of all the competition—and you might lose what could have been a strong offer.

- **Set the asking price exactly at the market value.** You may want to put your house on the market for exactly what it's worth. A fair price should generate genuine buyer interest. In a super-hot market, it may even bring in enough buyers to generate some price-raising competition. In a cooler market, it won't leave you much room to negotiate if you're really intent on getting your price, but that's still better than overpricing.

- **Set the asking price above market value.** As discussed above, some sellers' initial instinct is to start high, theoretically to leave room for negotiation. Just a tad above market value can work. A house that seems overpriced by a mere $10,000 won't drive away as many buyers as one that seems $50,000 too high—buyers are apt to think that you're willing to negotiate and haven't completely lost your mind when it comes to the home's actual value. (And if it's a $1.5 million home to begin with, a difference of $50,000 is not a big deal.) However, go too high and you'll lose buyers who assume your property is out of their range—or who don't even pick up on your listing during their online searches, when they choose a specific price range. You could even be helping your competition, by making their homes look reasonably priced by comparison.

What about a strategy of leaving your house on the market for a few months at a high price and waiting to get what you think it's worth? Unfortunately, the longer a house sits on the market, the less desirable it becomes. Buyers begin to wonder why it hasn't sold—did other buyers pick on some horrible flaw? Did past deals fall through for reasons to do with the seller? Pretty soon, you're lowering your price—perhaps dramatically.

Again, however, it's worth talking the list price decision over with your agent—and if you're feeling at all uncertain, perhaps getting a second opinion. "That's what I did before selling my home in Boston," says Carter. "As much as I respected my Realtor, I could tell that pricing a home involved not only science and data, but a certain amount of strategy and experience. I told the second Realtor up front that I wasn't going to use her services, to which she was agreeable. Interestingly, both Realtors came to very similar conclusions regarding my house's likely market value—but their strategy for getting buyers to offer that amount was very different. The Realtor I didn't use suggested putting the house on the market at exactly the amount we thought it was worth. My Realtor suggested listing it for $40,000 less, to bring in bidders. Her strategy worked: We got 11 solid offers from preapproved buyers, and the house sold for the amount we'd hoped for, with no inspection contingency."

What if the market value changes in the weeks during which you're preparing the house for sale? This, too, is important to take into account. Until the date your real estate agent enters the list price in the MLS, he or she should be keeping an eye out for any new comparables and reevaluating your home price accordingly. (That's why some real estate ads don't yet list a price.)

Best thing we ever did   **Accept the Realtor's suggestion to lower the list price based on updated comps.** "I was helping my 85-year old mother sell her townhouse, and we wanted it to move fast, since she'd already set a date to move into a retirement community," says Nell. "It took a few months to get the house in shape (lots of decluttering). By that time, the comps were trending lower, and our agent recommended we reduce the list price from what we'd originally planned. We reluctantly went along with this; a smart move, as it turned out. We received a full-price offer from the first buyers who visited. Several similar homes were for sale at the same time in my mother's development, but at higher prices. Those didn't sell for six months or more—and ultimately for less than we received. My mother was able to move when she wanted, and avoided having to double pay housing costs (including hefty homeowner association fees)."

$499,900 Versus $500,000: What's the Big Difference?

If you've ever looked online for a house—and according to the National Association of Realtors, a sizable majority of home buyers start their search that way—you've probably seen houses at prices hovering just below a seemingly huge number, like $499,900 instead of $500,000. It's not an unfamiliar tactic to consumers—after all, 99 cents still sounds cheaper (and is, slightly) than one dollar.

But there's an important reason home sellers do this, which extends beyond buyer psychology. Many online databases give buyers the option to look at homes in a certain price range: for example, between $475,000 and $499,999 ($25,000 price points are pretty common, both when setting database search criteria and in buyers' minds, when they think about how much they can afford). By pricing your home just below a cutoff amount, you can maximize the number of people looking at it, because buyers are usually willing to look *below* their maximum price points but not above them.

Websites, Open Houses, and Other Marketing Tools

The number of homes for sale is rising across the U.S., and you want yours to stand out. The more buyers who learn that it's for sale, the greater the odds that at least one of them will say, "Let's buy it!" That's where marketing comes in. While your agent will likely do most of the planning and hard work here, it's worth understanding the process and priorities, and getting involved at some points. (If you're selling FSBO, this will of course be a critical chapter for you to read and act upon.)

Your agent should have a ready task-list of marketing activities, which he or she will start carrying out as soon as you've signed the listing agreement. Some of these you may not even see in action, such as the agent talking up the house among fellow real estate pros. And plenty of agents come up with their own creative ideas, like the one who pitched a tent in the seller's front yard and kept his cell phone on so that he could show the place to buyers anytime, 24/7. Still, this is an area where your own creative thinking can help, too.

Let's assume that you and your agent will be working as a team to get your property viewed by as many prospective buyers as possible. This chapter will give you guidelines for how to carry out the basics, such as posting online ads and holding an open house, as well as ideas for going above and beyond the usual marketing strategies.

> **CAUTION**
>
> **Typos and other errors happen.** Whether you or your agent prepares written marketing materials, it's best to run everything past a second—or even third—pair of eyes. We know of at least one case where the agent posted an open-house ad with the wrong address! Other sellers have been unhappy with the house photos or caught errors in the house description. Ask to see the marketing material in advance.

Knowing Your Audience

First things first. As you take the steps recommended below, we suggest you keep someone specific in mind: your buyer. While you obviously don't know who that is yet, you can probably make some educated guesses. In a small condominium in the middle of a busy city and close to public transportation, your buyer is most likely to be a working professional, possibly single. If you're selling a rambler in a suburb with excellent schools and a park nearby, it's likely to draw a family with school-aged children.

Who's Currently Looking to Buy a Home?

In preparing to sell, it helps to have a picture of your most likely buyer in mind. You can probably make some educated guesses based on the demographics of who's already living in your neighborhood, and what the locality has to offer. The following 2013 statistics from the National Association of Realtors may also offer some insights to help you target your marketing efforts:

- Around 38% of 2013 buyers were purchasing their first home. (Remember what that was like?)
- The average age of first-time buyers was 31, the typical repeat buyer was 52, and the overall average age of buyers was 42.
- Median income among first-time buyers was $63,000, with $96,000 for repeat buyers and an overall median of $83,300.
- Around 66% of home buyers in 2013 were married couples. Single female buyers comprised 16% of buyers, and single men, 9%.
- In 40% of homebuyers' households there lived children under the age of 18.
- Saving for a down payment was cited as difficult by 12% of buyers, due in particular to student loans, credit card debt, and car loans.
- Ninety-six percent of home buyers speak English.

Source: 2013 "Profile of Home Buyers and Sellers."

Why bother thinking about this? Because you may be able to tailor some of your marketing material to your audience. While you can't expect to cover every prospect, it's worth spending a little time thinking about who will be coming through most frequently and making the marketing material—not to mention the house itself—as attractive to those buyers as possible.

> **CAUTION**
>
> **Don't discriminate.** Federal (and often state or local) fair housing laws prohibit you from discriminating against potential buyers based on factors like race, color, national origin, religion, sex, familial status, or disability. While you may market your house with the general idea that it will probably appeal to a certain type of buyer, your marketing materials shouldn't say that's who you're seeking.

How Would You Describe Your House's Most Likely Buyer?

Start by thinking about your home's attractive features, then who will be drawn to them. Here are some objective factors; your home itself will no doubt reveal similar clues:

- **Size.** A house with many bedrooms will probably draw families with children; a smaller house may draw empty-nesters or young singles.
- **Schools.** A good school district is most important to families with children (though it holds general appeal because it affects resale value).
- **Location.** In a suburb or small town, expect buyers who are looking for a quiet place to live. In the city, you may get more people seeking cultural activity and nightlife. Proximity to recreational facilities, public transport, and places to work will also influence your pool of likely buyers.
- **Layout.** A house with stairs, for example, will have less appeal for a retiring couple or for families with small children, who may prefer the convenience and safety of one level.
- **Condition.** If your house is completely remodeled and needs no fixups, it's just right for someone looking to spend time doing other things—perhaps a driven, working professional who's

looking for a low-maintenance place. (That's someone who might be drawn by an extra bedroom that's staged as a home office.) On the other hand, if your house needs some fixing up and the price reflects it, it will probably appeal more to people on a budget (such as first-time buyers).

- **Price range.** If your house will be priced at less than the median for your area, you'll more likely be dealing with first-time buyers breaking into the market. This is especially true if you're also in an area with lots of other first-time buyers—for example, a subdivision of small "starter" homes.

By using this list and thinking of other special features about your home, as well as the demographics of where you live, you should be able to narrow in on a few groups likely to buy your house. It may be that your house appeals to multiple groups: For example, its location in a good school district might make it ideal for families with children, while the condominium ownership structure might make it ideal for single professionals who travel a lot.

Matching Your Marketing Efforts to Your Buyer

What's the secret to making your marketing plan and materials attract the folks you identified as likely buyers? Consider customizing the following:

- **Written descriptions of the property.** Although your marketing material must accurately reflect your home, you also want it to highlight the features of greatest interest to your prospective purchasers. If, for instance, you're selling a small two-bedroom house in a vibrant, diverse neighborhood, you may want to mention the flexibility of the second bedroom, which could be used for an office, guest room, or nursery.
- **Ad placements.** In an area likely to draw families looking for good schools, placing an ad in a neighborhood paper or even at the school might be appropriate.
- **Online presentation of the property.** For buyers looking for a bustling community, don't forget to include a shot of the busy weekend farmer's market in a nearby park. Or, if your home

may appeal to unrelated folks sharing space—perhaps because it's a townhouse with two master suites, or in a college town—be sure to include pictures of both bedrooms and bathrooms, and emphasize the privacy-enhancing features.

- **Property staging.** Talk to your stager (if you hire one) about who you think will be visiting the house, and how the staging can boost the house's appeal to those people. For example, if you live in a thriving artist's community, you might stage a semifinished garage to look like an artist's studio.

- **Time of sale.** Obviously, if you need to sell, you need to sell. But if you have some control over when it happens, targeting times of year best suited to your buying audience may be effective. For example, in a college town, turnover may be highest at the end of summer or beginning of fall, when students are just returning or arriving. (Along with students come professors, support staff, and perhaps graduate or mature students who may already be thinking about buying.) And families will want to move before the school year starts, to help kids adjust to new schools.

- **Buyer incentives.** If the market happens to be slow in your area, you may want to consider offering incentives to your prospective buyer. If you're in a starter home, seller financing (discussed later in this chapter) may look particularly attractive to first-time buyers who have a hard time qualifying for a loan. If you're in a more upscale neighborhood, prospective buyers may already own their own homes and be more appreciative if you're willing to accept a home-sale contingency (meaning they don't have to close the deal on your home until they've sold theirs).

Maximizing Your House's Online Exposure

The vast majority of buyers start their search for homes online. Why, after all, should buyers go driving around and traipsing through every single home in their price range?

This creates both an opportunity and a hurdle for you. You have the opportunity to put interesting visual images of your house in front of countless people, even the ones who happen to be wearing pajamas at the time. But virtual images can also turn off some buyers; for example, a buyer may tell her agent, "I already saw that one online—and don't like the look of that tiny back yard, so let's skip it."

Obviously, you want your house's online presentation to make a buyer anxious for a personal visit, not anxious to look elsewhere. Here's how to best achieve that.

Get Your House on the Right Websites

One of the most important parts of making sure your house reaches potential buyers is ensuring that it's on websites that buyers actually visit. Here's where to start:

- **The local MLS.** The Multiple Listing Service (MLS) is a local or regional database of available homes for sale. Real estate agents almost always post their clients' homes on the MLS, where other agents can access important details. (They'll do this a week or two before the house goes on the market.) The information from MLS systems is also often accessible, in limited form, to the public.

- **Realtor.com.** The information in local MLS databases drives data to many other online sources. The most prominent of these is www.realtor.com, the website for the National Association of Realtors (NAR), which aggregates listings from around the country and is a popular search tool for many potential homebuyers.

- **Your real estate agent's website.** Your real estate agent will probably have a personal or company website, which should include your listing. In fact, it should give your listing greater exposure than the MLS and other websites might allow for, with lots of photos, a virtual tour, and so on. If either the agent or the brokerage highlight specific properties—for example, by listing them as "featured," find out what it takes to get the special designation.

- **A website created especially for your home.** Many agents will create a website just for your home, with its own URL, such as www.950parkerstreet.com. Alternatively, the agent may just purchase the domain name and steer the site to the listing on his or her website. This again offers a great opportunity to market your property without space limitations—that is, to post as many pictures as you want (without facing the limits imposed by the MLS), or with as much detailed description as you'd like. Find out whether your agent offers this service, or be prepared to do it yourself. A blog is a simple alternative.

- **Other popular real estate websites.** Many websites draw information from MLS systems automatically, and your agent hopefully shares listings with other agents, as well. That means you shouldn't have to do anything extra to make sure your house appears on such websites as Zillow, Trulia, Yahoo! Homes, Redfin, and FrontDoor. Check with your real estate agent to be certain.

> **TIP**
>
> **Raise your Zestimate by claiming your home on Zillow.** As the owner of a home, you have the unique right to go into Zillow's influential website and augment its description of your home—and possibly raise its "Zestimate" accordingly. This estimate of your home's value is created by computers, which lack feet and eyeballs with which to visit your house. The result can be way off. First, check your Zestimate to see what dollar figure buyers will be looking at: Will they come to your house thinking it's a bargain (or that maybe you've priced it low because of hidden problems), or that it's overpriced? In either case, it's worth taking follow-up steps. On the Zillow listing page for your home, click the link for "Correct home facts." Then, you will be prompted to create an account and verify your ownership. Once registered, you can amend the basic information offered, such as number of bedrooms and baths, type of flooring, included appliances, and so on. This still can't possibly account for factors like a great location, a tree-lined street, a great layout, or a stunning remodel, but it's a start.

- **Your home stager's website, if you hire one.** Your home stager will have good reason to post pictures of your home. It's a great example of the work the stager can do and is likely to appeal to

prospective clients. But the increased online exposure is good
for you, too.

- **Craigslist.org.** This free service is popular for everything from
selling cars and furniture to, that's right, houses. (Look for
"real estate for sale.") Your agent should be able to create the
posting for you and may be able to link in a series of photos or
a virtual tour.

- **Local newspaper.** Your local newspaper may list homes for sale
online, either through the local MLS or because you've bought
a print or online classified ad.

Making Sure Your House Looks Good Onscreen

When posting pictures of your home online, you want to highlight its
best features without giving a completely inaccurate view of the place.
(If that sounds obvious, take a look online to see how many home
sellers violate it, on sites like http://terriblerealestateagentphotos.com.)
And stay out of the pictures yourself!

Your agent (if you work with one) will likely take the marketing
pictures or hire a professional to do so. Either of these options is
probably better than taking the pictures yourself, because people
who do it frequently will know what works best.

Lesson learned the hard way **Wish I'd checked my agent's photographic abilities beforehand.** Marie was mostly happy with her agent's aesthetic instincts. The agent offered many tips for making the place look good, so that they didn't have to spend money on a stager. "But she fell down on the job when it came to photos," says Marie. "We didn't see them until they were already published, unfortunately. They were just bad—dark, and amateurish."

The major downside to hiring a professional photographer is that if
it rains or is overcast on the scheduled day for shooting, you probably
won't get the best possible images. Try to build in some flexibility for
rescheduling. Also make sure you'll get enough notice of the photo shoot
to clean and prepare your house without having to fly into a panic.

Whether you take pictures yourself or hire someone else to do it, make sure:

- **You've already cleaned, decluttered, and staged if that's part of your plans.** Don't take pictures until you've taken the steps described in Chapter 5 to make your house buyer ready.

- **It's light and bright.** Indoor pictures should be taken in the middle of the day, preferably on a sunny day. Open all window coverings and make sure windows are clean, to let maximum natural light in. Outdoor shots usually work best when the sun is at your back.

- **You choose the right angle.** A professional will have experience identifying the best vantage points; if you're doing the shooting yourself, you'll probably have to move around and try different angles.

- **You choose the rooms and features that buyers most want to see.** Outside, you'll want a picture of the front of your home (without one, buyers will suspect that your home is ugly, and may dismiss it quickly) and then a backyard shot or two—more if you have a nice patio or grass area or attractive landscaping. Inside, start with the room most important to buyers—the kitchen. If yours is modern and upgraded, you'll definitely want a shot or two of it. Then move to common areas buyers will want to see, plus at least a bedroom or two. And if your bathroom is particularly attractive, for example because it's larger than average or recently remodeled, you'll want a shot of that too.

One step up from pictures is a video or "virtual tour." Many real estate agents have the programs needed to create these "tours," or use services such as Visualtour.com or RealTour Fusion. These tours allow buyers to get a moving picture of your home, as if walking between the various rooms, and thus learning how they're all connected. Virtual tours are typically accompanied by background music (of the soothing, generic sort) and sometimes a voiceover.

Make sure your agent plans to post multiple pictures of your home on the local MLS and any other places where your home will be viewed online. Many agents do this as a standard part of their marketing plan, but it's worth asking for specifics. In some cases, putting up more than a minimum number of photos will cost the agent extra—but it could be money well spent.

Create an Enticing Online Description

In addition to the pictures, your online posting should include a description of your property. Again, your real estate agent will write this, but ask to see it before it goes up. You're looking for:

- **Accuracy.** If your house has three bedrooms and two bathrooms, that's obviously how you'll want it advertised. Also check the lot size, square footage, address, directions, school district, and other factual details. (If your agent presents wrong information now, it could work its way into more official documents later—and buyers have sued sellers for things like overstating the home's square footage.)
- **Focus on your home's best features.** Your agent should zero in on what's best about your home, whether it's the open floor plan, remodeled kitchen, or picturesque back yard. If you think particular features bear special mention, bring these up with your agent.
- **Code words.** Real estate professionals use "code words" that carry specific meaning—for example, "motivated seller" or "bring all offers" tells other agents and buyers that the seller is anxious to sell and willing to consider offers below asking price. If that's true and you don't mind sharing the information with the buyer, no problem. But if you're more focused on getting top dollar than selling quickly, nix this language and ask your agent to decipher any other words that look coded.
- **The commission split.** Seller's agents usually split the commission 50/50 with the buyer's agent. If you have anything different planned, it should be reflected in the listing.

Other Ways of Getting the Word Out

In addition to the virtual world, you and your real estate agent will likely want to employ a number of real-world marketing strategies, such as the below.

Create a Listing Sheet

A listing sheet is a flyer you will distribute to interested buyers, make available at open houses, and perhaps put in a flyer box on your yard sign (discussed below). Your agent should create this for you. To get an idea of what's usually on your agent's listing sheets, ask for a sample first.

The basic principle to remember is that the listing sheet isn't just a recitation of your house and its features. It's an advertisement, designed to draw in buyers. It should highlight your home's best features with both descriptive and factual text. For example, instead of stating "backyard garden and spa," you might say, "outdoor retreat with Zen garden and luxury spa" (unless it's just an ancient hot tub with algae growing in it).

The listing sheet should include pictures—in color, to maximize contrast and appearance.

Get Other Agents Excited About Your House

Your agent isn't the only one trying to sell your house. In all likelihood, local buyers' agents are just as eager to find the perfect match between your property and their clients. But with an increasing number of properties on the market, you still want to make sure your house gets prospective buyers' full attention and stays on their minds.

Start by making sure your agent does a special open house for other agents (sometimes called a "broker's tour"). This is an opportunity for the real estate community to come look at your property (usually on a weekday) and for each agent to decide whether your home could meet any clients' criteria. If it does, the agent will come back for repeat visits and bring clients along.

These open houses can create a buzz about your house. A number of agents will be in there all at once, and many of them already know each other. They'll be sharing opinions with the raucousness of movie reviewers, from "This kitchen will sell the place," to "Oh no, what were they thinking with the fuchsia bathroom tile?" If your house is well priced and looks great, they may be vying to bring purchasing clients in quickly.

Yes, People Will Be in Your House, Touching Your Things

"When you put a house on the market, it's open to the public," reminds Bellevue-based Realtor Patricia Wangsness. "People won't be eating at your table, but they may be sitting on your couch, walking on newly vacuumed carpet, and so on. Some sellers get very uncomfortable with this. I knew one seller who would fold the toilet paper in a special way so she'd know if someone had used the bathroom! One once told me, 'Someone touched my bedspread!' Try to remember that you are trying to sell the place, and people are not going to buy it until they can feel that it can be theirs."

Speaking of repeat visits, make sure it's easy for agents to make them. The most practical thing is for your agent to leave a lockbox on the front door—a small box that can be opened with a special key or a code, which professional agents will have. With very little notice, this allows prospective buyers to come over and have a look around. This works well any time of day, so if your agent can't be available to open the place up on a regular basis, a buyer's agent can just call and ask for permission to take a client on a tour. Of course, it also requires you to keep your house in good shape at virtually all times—something we recommend anyway when you're trying to sell.

CAUTION

Make sure your agent promptly returns calls and other inquiries.
Even with a foolproof system for allowing potential purchasers to look at
your home, you also need an agent committed to getting them in the door.
Before hiring, discuss with your agent how long it will take to respond to buyer
inquiries. Also make sure your agent solicits feedback from other agents after
visits to your home and shares that feedback with you.

Hold a Public Open House

Open houses are a standard in most real estate agents' marketing
portfolios, but grudgingly: The word among agents is that open
houses rarely lead to sales. Also, they can be expensive to advertise,
and most of the people coming through are just lookers not ready to
make a decision, or neighbors and other homeowners checking out
the competition.

Nevertheless, keeping maximum traffic going through your house
can increase the odds of a sale—and there's still the possibility that
someone who visits an open house will come back to buy, or make a
recommendation to a friend who's also looking. Unless your agent points
to specific reasons that an open house makes no sense in your local
market, it's worth the limited amount of time it takes. Just recognize
that if you get few visitors, it's probably not worth doing another one;
that's an indicator that in your market, you're probably better off having
your agent allocate marketing time and money elsewhere.

TIP

**Make sure your agent advertises your open house in your MLS
listing.** That way, other agents and prospective buyers know they can visit.

Your agent should plan to hold at least one open house, and
possibly more. (You can always cancel a scheduled open house if
you find an acceptable offer beforehand.) Your main responsibilities
before the open house are cleaning and sprucing up (as described in
Chapter 5) and then getting yourself, your family, and your pets out

for the day. Your agent is the best one to interact with visitors. The agent will also want to set out written materials for buyers to look at or take away, including copies of the listing sheet, inspection reports or disclosures (if customarily provided in your state), press clippings about the neighborhood, and the like.

Best thing we ever did

Hold a second open house. "We put our house on the market in November," says Florence, "knowing this was a slow time. But my husband had found a job across the country, so we had to move. After the first open house, we received one so-so offer, and were considering accepting it. Our agent wasn't hopeful about holding another open house, but we went ahead with it after she found a fellow agent to be there that day. (I think he was hoping to pick up clients.) A couple came in who'd only just begun thinking about buying a home. It was the first place they'd looked at. They fell in love with it, made a stronger offer than the first one, and we were in escrow by the following Thursday."

Hold a Specially Themed Open House

The standard open house isn't your only possibility. Creative home sellers have come up with variations on the theme—sometimes called "extreme open houses"—based on their house's particular features. This might be something that your agent arranges and pays for, if your home is sufficiently high-end to warrant such an investment. For example, one of Bellevue-based agents Patricia and David Wangsness's signature events is called Rendering the Possibilities.™ As Patricia explains, "We take a home that needs renovation, perhaps an older house in a good neighborhood. Then we bring in a designer and a contractor to look at what can be done with the place. They set up drawing boards and write up estimates. That way, visiting home buyers can get an expert look at the home's potential and what it will cost to realize."

Other sellers with large backyards good for entertaining have held barbecues, or arranged for musicians to entertain visitors. Creative sellers have hired professional chefs to create (and serve) gourmet dishes to show off a remodeled kitchen, or put up an art or antiques show in coordination with a local gallery or shop.

Events like these can, if poorly planned, admittedly cross the line into being gimmicky, and may not always be worth you or your agent spending a lot of money on. Nevertheless, it's worth giving some thought to how you might make your open house stand out, either at the public open house or the broker's tour. And if there's already an architect, chef, musician, or other relevant professional in your circle of friends and family, why not create an event that people will make a special effort to attend?

Get Into Print Advertising

Whether it's worth your agent's limited advertising budget to get your property into physical print is questionable and depends on where you live. In most places, users will go online first. Even if they later pick up a description of your house in a classified ad, it's not going to have the same impact that multiple images would.

However, a few newspapers still have robust real estate sections, often with a special pullout on weekends. Or, small local papers may be the place that interested buyers look first, with affordable advertising and lots of space for photos. If your house can be featured in one of these, it might be worth paying for. But if all you're getting is a three-line classified ad, you'll find it tough to draw much attention, especially if the ad is full of cryptic abbreviations. If you're going to do such an ad, focus especially on appealing adjectives that will help buyers picture what they can't see.

Like newspapers, other print media—magazines, local circulars, and the like—rarely sell homes. Your agent may still use these forms of advertising, but don't expect big results. You're better off working with an agent who will focus primarily on promoting your house online.

Put Up a Yard Sign

A yard sign is a simple yet effective tool for letting others know your property is for sale—or at least for confirming to someone following up on their online search that, "Yes, this is the place." People who live in the neighborhood will see it, and perhaps spread the word to friends, family, and colleagues. Your agent will provide the sign—in literal terms, will likely send someone to hammer it into your front yard. (If you don't have an agent, see Chapter 11 for more tips on putting up signs.)

If your agent has created a custom website for your house, you can provide the URL on a "rider"—the small plaque that hangs off the bottom of the sign. Riders can also be used for information like open house hours. Also make sure the relevant phone number is visible; if it's a custom extension number (with a prerecorded message, for example), be sure the extension is also on the sign.

Your sign should be visible from the street (that is, perpendicular to it) so anyone driving by can read the details—most importantly, the contact information. (While you'll get some people walking by, most local foot traffic isn't house hunting.) Also consider having a flyer box to hold your listing sheet (discussed above). Just recognize that you'll need to keep it regularly stocked. Ask your agent to leave extra copies at your house, so you can refill it as needed.

TIP

There's a reason your agent won't take the sign down until the closing. If you're living in the home and get tired of seeing curious passersby checking out your home, you might wish the "For Sale" sign could be taken down as soon as you're in contract with a buyer. But a lot can go wrong during the escrow period, such that you have to re-list your home. That's why agents ordinarily leave the sign up. But if the agent hasn't hung a "Sale Pending" rider from the bottom of the sign, you can certainly ask for that.

Get the Word Out to People You Know

It isn't unheard of to meet the person who buys your house through a common acquaintance. In fact, using your current personal contacts can be a good way to augment your agent's marketing efforts. (But if you signed the standard listing agreement, you'll still need to pay the agent a commission.)

Start by letting your immediate circle know you're putting the place up for sale. Post the link to your website on Facebook, and announce your coming sale on any neighborhood listservs such as "NextDoor."

Pass around your listing sheet, website address, or other property description. Send an email or postcard to everyone you know who may be of use—most likely, neighbors and nearby family and friends. (Some real estate agents will send postcards to neighbors as a regular part of their marketing plan.) Explain that you're selling and are interested in finding someone through your current contacts. Ask them to forward the link or other information to anyone they know looking for a home in the area.

Open the search up to anyone and everyone you can think of, from your dentist to the gardener to the neighbor you've never met. Encourage others to pass the information along, and make sure it's easy for any interested party to reach your real estate agent or you (especially if you're unrepresented).

Best thing we ever did **Announce on NextDoor that I was seeking boxes for moving.** "I didn't even mention that were planning to sell," says Cathy. "But a neighbor who's also a real estate agent read between the lines and got in touch with my agent. She brought in a buyer who loved the place, and we ended up arranging a sale without us having to do any of the repairs, staging, and open houses we'd been planning!"

Hold a Neighbors' Open House

Your agent will probably plan on doing an open house for local agents and another for the public. You might also talk to your agent about holding an open house just for the neighbors (with or without your agent's presence). This lets people nearby know that they're free to come poking around your place. And you may get some good feedback or leads.

Consider serving light snacks or drinks. Put balloons outside the front door to attract attention and make the place feel festive and welcoming. You can keep the mood light, since you're not actively trying to sell to someone who lives in the neighborhood. (Of course, if a neighbor shows interest, be sure you provide information on how to contact your agent.)

Financial Incentives for Buyers

If you're in an area where the market is slow or where the average buyer has trouble qualifying for financing, you can improve your home's sales prospects by offering various financial incentives as part of your marketing efforts, including:

- acting as the lender yourself, for part or all of the home's selling price (minus down payment)
- contributing cash or paying points so the buyer can get a better interest rate on a bank loan, or
- offering a lease option, in which the prospective buyer rents the house while saving up to purchase it.

How Seller Financing Works

A buyer who has only 10% to put down, for example, and can find a bank that will lend 80% of the purchase price might be able to complete the sale if you fund the 10% difference (as a "second mortgage").

You won't literally hand cash to the buyer—instead, you'll extend credit to the buyer at the closing. In return, you'll get a deed of trust or a mortgage, which means if the buyer doesn't pay you back, you can foreclose on the property.

For as long as you're the lender, the buyer is obligated to make regular monthly payments to you. These payments will likely comprise both interest and principal, so you'll be earning money. But of course, you'll walk away with less cash at closing, so this option works best if you own your house outright, have a lot of equity built up in it, or for some other reason don't need all the cash from the sale immediately.

Seller-financed loans are frequently short term—say, three to five years—with a balloon payment due at the end. This allows the buyer some time to get financially stable then refinance with a traditional lender when his or her financial picture looks a little better. Hopefully, the buyer's income or credit will go up, the buyer will accrue some serious equity, or a combination of these factors will occur.

TIP

Don't wait for buyers to request seller financing. While some may be brave enough to broach this topic, you can open the door by adding the words "Seller financing available" to your MLS listing. You might also attach a rider to your For Sale sign that reads "Seller Financing."

Seller Financing Is Not for the Faint of Heart: Get Help

Because there is substantial risk involved in seller financing, before you sign on the dotted line you'll need to do a thorough review of the buyer's finances and credit history and evaluate the likelihood that you'll get your money back if the buyer defaults (which involves predicting how much your home's value will increase in the short term, among other things). Most people need the help of an attorney or other professional to decipher credit reports, run the buyer's debt-to-income ratios, and the like.

Once you are satisfied that the buyer is a good credit risk, you'll need to draft a promissory note and mortgage or deed of trust in order to seal the deal and then "record" the mortgage with the proper office. These documents can be quite detailed and complex, and if you don't draw them up or record them correctly, you might lose the right to go after the buyer for repayment if he or she later defaults. This is one area where you definitely need the assistance of a real estate attorney. Your real estate agent will likely be able to recommend someone.

Probably the biggest disadvantage to seller financing is that if the buyer doesn't pay up, you'll have to foreclose on the property to try to get your cash out. The expense and hassle of the foreclosure process can be a lot to take on. Even worse, if you're in a secondary position to the primary lender (which will almost always be the case unless you're the sole lender), you might not be able to recover all (or possibly any) of what you're owed. This is because the foreclosure sale proceeds will first cover the costs of foreclosure and then the balance of the primary lender's loan. You get what's left over, if anything.

Even if the buyer is paying you on time, if he or she defaults on payments to the primary lender, that lender will likely foreclose. Again, if there's nothing left after the bank gets paid, you'll be out of luck.

How Buying Down the Interest Rate Works

Another increasingly popular incentive is for the seller to contribute cash with which the buyer can "buy down" the interest rate. There are two ways to do this: a temporary buydown, in which you pay part of the buyer's interest obligation in the short term (say, three years), or a more permanent buydown. With the more permanent buydown, you essentially pay "points" on the buyer's mortgage. Points are an up-front cash payment, expressed as a percentage of the loan balance—for example, one point on a $200,000 loan is $2,000. The more points the buyer pays, the lower the interest rate, resulting in long-term savings over the life of the loan and smaller monthly payments. And if you pay some of the points, it might even help the buyer get a loan.

How Lease-to-Own Arrangements Work

Even in a market where buyers have lots of good deals to pick from, some may not yet feel sure they're ready. Maybe a prospective buyer is finishing school and would love to settle down in the area, but figures it will take a few years to build up a down payment. Or perhaps the buyer is new to the area and is thinking about buying, but is still not quite sure.

To reel in such buyers (or if you already have a tenant in your home who's hoping to buy someday), you may want to offer a lease option. Here's how it works. For starters, the interested party would lease your home from you, much like an ordinary rental. However, the lease would include the opportunity to buy the place at or by some set date in the future. As part of the deal, the prospective buyer would pay you something—either an up-front fee, or more likely a monthly amount, in addition to the rent—for the right to the option.

Lease options are particularly appealing to buyers who think the market is going to heat up soon but can't yet make a purchase. The buyer can lock in a low price, then decide a couple of years later (by which time, according to the buyer's hopes, your house's value will have exceeded the preset price) whether to exercise the option and buy your home.

Of course, as the seller, you'll get less on the deal than you would have by waiting and offering the property for sale at the higher value, years down the line. But this strategy may ultimately get your house sold, and in the meantime, you get the regular monthly rent, plus whatever extra the buyer agrees to pay you for the value of the lease option. And if the buyer ultimately decides not to buy the place, you can (hopefully) sell it at a higher price, plus pocket the money you were paid for the option.

Lease options can, however, create a few headaches. For example:

- **You become a landlord.** You'll have to collect rent, maintain the property, buy necessary insurance, and more. And the tenant may not care for your house as lovingly as you did.
- **There may be tax implications.** For example, if you wait too long to sell, you may end up owing capital gains tax. Discuss this and other tax implications with your tax adviser.
- **You can lose any appreciation in value.** If your house appreciates over the years it's occupied as a rental, but you've already set an option price, you won't get the benefit of the gain when the buyer decides to exercise the option.
- **You won't get much immediate cash.** While you'll get something for the value of the option, plus rental income, you won't immediately get the proceeds of your sale.

CAUTION

Get help from a real estate attorney. If you plan to do a lease option, you'll need to draw up an agreement that includes typical terms of a standard lease as well as language that specifically covers the option. It's important to get the language right in order to avoid problems down the line. Get help from a real estate professional or attorney.

Receiving and Evaluating Offers

Before long, one or more buyers will hopefully decide that your house is worth making an offer on. Time to high-five your real estate agent—your marketing efforts worked, and the home is attracting buyer interest.

The next question is whether the buyer's offer is one you'll want to accept, based on factors such as price, contingencies, the solidity of the buyer's financing, and so on. And if you're lucky enough to receive multiple offers for your house (as is now common in many parts of the U.S.), you'll need to compare all these factors among the offers, so as to choose the best one.

> **TIP**
>
> **What if you aren't getting any offers?** It's possible your house isn't being marketed well (as discussed in Chapter 7) or, more likely, it's overpriced. Review Chapter 6 and talk to your agent about whether to make a price adjustment. If 30 days have passed with no offers, act quickly to reduce the price—by at least $10,000 if you're to attract any attention.

When and How You Will Receive Offers

To present the offer, the buyer's agent will get in touch with your agent and possibly arrange to meet. In a hot market where you expect multiple offers, your agent may add structure to the process, likely by setting a deadline for offers or a time that the buyers' agents can present offers in person. Your agent may then schedule the buyers' agents for limited time slots in quick succession, perhaps on a weekday evening.

Before such an offer meeting or deadline, your agent's phone will be ringing and emails pinging nonstop. That's because the various buyers' agents will want up-to-the-minute information on how many offers are expected. Your agent can't give them any details of what's in those other offers (and may not even have that information yet), but he or she is expected to at least tell buyers' agents how many people have expressed serious interest, for example by requesting a full packet of disclosure information. That helps those buyers still writing up offers to decide how far out on a limb to go in making theirs stand out.

You may want to attend the offer presentation meeting. It's a great opportunity to not only get the news as soon as your agent does, but to get a sense of the personality of the agent with whom your agent will be dealing on a regular basis if you enter into a contract. The buyers are unlikely to attend these presentation meetings.

What the Buyer's Offer Will Look Like

The real estate industry has developed standard practices for how a buyer will submit an offer to you. Because these practices vary by state, we can't tell you exactly what form the buyer's offer will take. Not to worry, your real estate agent will know the process well. (If selling FSBO, contact your state's department of real estate to get information on how things are handled.)

You will most likely receive the offer in writing, on a standard form created by your state's Realtor association. These forms typically include not only the buyer's proposed price, but the conditions (contingencies) that must be met for the deal to finalize, the procedures for resolving any disputes between the buyer and you, specification of who will pay what fees (such as for the escrow, title, or other closing fees), and many other details. Ask your agent or attorney to carefully review all of these with you.

In many states, such as California, the standard written offer is so comprehensive that you'd simply need to sign it (and perhaps have an attorney review it) for it to serve as a complete purchase contract. Of course, you'd want to review the document carefully before doing this, because it's full of important terms worth understanding. (See Chapter 10 for a clause-by-clause rundown of what's in a standard purchase contract.)

In a few states, however, the standard offer is a very short document that simply communicates a wish to buy the house at a certain price. The buyer then waits for you, the seller, to create the first draft of the purchase agreement (with help from your real estate agent or attorney). These offers may even be oral, rather than written. That's okay, but only a written sales contract is valid, so at some point, you'll both have to sign on the dotted line.

How Tough a Negotiator Should You Be?

With the hot market currently sweeping much of the U.S., you may, as a seller, find yourself in the stronger negotiating position. If the buyer doesn't like the deal you're offering, you can probably find another one—possibly even a better one—very soon.

How far can you take this power? There's actually a lot to be said for closing the deal with the buyer you start out with. The longer it takes to sell your house, the longer you will be paying for utilities (regardless of whether you're there or have moved on), insurance, rental of any staging furniture (depending on the length of your agreement with the stager), your mortgage, and perhaps homeowners' association fees. This is especially true if you are paying an additional mortgage on your next home. Also, if you're eager to move on because of a new job cross-country or some other external life factor, the buyer is likely to get wind of this, and might apply pressure accordingly.

Nevertheless, you can enjoy the benefits of having some leverage. Perhaps you will negotiate for concessions you might never have received from buyers while the market was cold—like a provision allowing you to remain in the home for a month or two after the closing (perhaps even rent-free!) to give you time to buy or move into your next abode.

Beyond the paperwork, buyers' agents may make a small presentation. Each agent will give a summary of the buyer's offer, highlighting its strong features and downplaying its weak ones (for example, "Even if this isn't the highest offer you receive today, look at how big the down payment is! My clients will have no trouble getting final loan approval"). The agent will try to give you a sense of the buyers as people ("They're a lovely couple whose hobby is gardening, and they're so excited that your yard already has mature fruit trees"). The agent might also submit letters or even short videos from or about the buyer. The idea is to give you a sense that you'll be choosing new owners for your home who will be responsible and easy to work with as you bring the deal to a close, and will take good care of and enjoy your home in the coming years.

Lesson learned the hard way **"I was way more influenced by the buyer letters than I expected."** According to Maggie, "We received a whopping ten offers on our Oakland home, so the competition was fierce. When my agent first told me that buyers might write us personal letters, I thought, 'How cheesy, as if that would change my mind about which one to select!' But then, listening to the offer presentations, I found myself thinking things like, 'What a nice young couple, he's a teacher and she works at a nonprofit, I so want them to live in our house!' Thank goodness the highest offer also came from an incredibly lovely and community-minded young couple."

I Like That One!
Choosing Among Competing Offers

If you're evaluating competing offers, you'll want to consider not only the price, but other factors, including:
- the buyers' financial ability to close the deal
- any contingencies or other terms attached to the offer, and
- the reputation of the buyers' agent for fair and intelligent dealing.

After over 30 years' experience as a real estate broker, Carol Neil says, "The best price is not necessarily the best offer. You want an offer that will close escrow, and close near to the offer price." Even if one offer is clearly the highest in price, it instantly becomes less attractive if other factors might get in the way of the deal going through—for example, if the buyer's agent is known for being an uncompromising negotiator or for nickeling and diming sellers after the inspection report comes back. That's likely to bring down the dollar value of the offer in the all-too-near future.

How much time will you have in which to evaluate each offer before responding? Check the offer itself, which should specify a date and time when it will automatically expire. Some buyers put short expiration dates on their offers, to try to push you into action or beat out other buyers. Don't let this unnerve you. If you need more time to consider the offer, your agent can contact theirs and ask whether they're still going to be interested later. They probably will be.

Should You Consider a Preemptive Offer?

To avoid joining in on a likely bidding war, some buyers try to get in early, with what's called a "preemptive offer." This is typically made either before the property is listed for sale or before the date you've specified for hearing offers. To make the offer so tempting that you won't be inclined to look further, the buyer will ordinarily name a high price and include other attractive terms—perhaps all cash (no financing contingency) or a waiver of the inspection contingency.

You might indeed be tempted by a preemptive offer. If you like everything about it, and can't imagine receiving a better one, then perhaps it's worth accepting.

But many sellers' agents counsel against accepting preemptive offers, as a matter of policy. For one thing, it's not fair to other buyers, who thought they had until a particular date to prepare their offers. What's more, accepting this first offer means you'll never know whether you could have gotten an even better one by waiting—and the wait might be only a matter of days, depending on how far along you are in the process. Besides, if the preemptive offerors loved your house enough to attempt this strategy, chances are they're not going to disappear. They'll be right there, bidding alongside everyone else when the time comes.

Evaluating the Financial Parts of the Offer

The envelope please: You're probably dying to see what price your prospective buyer or buyers have offered. But that's not all you should look at, even when evaluating money issues. There's lots of other relevant financial information within the typical offer.

First Things First: The Price

If you're offered your asking price, let out a cheer. That means you assessed the market well, and at least one buyer agrees that the house is worth that much. Perhaps you'll even be offered more than that amount—an especially likely scenario if buyers know that multiple offers were expected.

> (!) CAUTION
>
> **No matter the price, every noncash offer has to pass the appraisal test.** Although one or more buyers may be willing to pay more than the asking price, their lenders could refuse to finance the loan where the agreed-upon price (or at least the loan amount) is higher than the property's appraised value. For more on this issue, see the discussion of "Getting Past the Appraisal Contingency" in Chapter 10.

What if the first offer you receive is less than your asking price? If it's at the lower end of what you'd expected or hoped to get, and no other visitors have shown much interest, it might be worth considering. Waiting for a higher offer could risk the house going stale on the market, and will add to your costs—especially if you've already moved out and have to keep paying utilities, homeowners' association fees, and a mortgage on your empty house, not to mention rental fees on furniture. But check the comparables again, and have a serious talk with your agent. Counteroffering at closer to your asking price might be worth a try.

TIP

It's okay to feel annoyed at buyers who offer less because of their remodeling plans. You may encounter prospective buyers who have the mistaken idea that they can reduce their offer price by whatever amount they're going to need to, say, redo the kitchen to their taste, or construct an addition. A buyer's plans for your property have nothing to do with its inherent value. Assuming your house was priced appropriately for its current condition, you should feel justified in rejecting an artificially low offer.

Earnest-Money Deposit

The buyer's offer may be accompanied by a sum of money (probably in the form of a check) called an earnest-money or good-faith deposit. The idea is that a buyer who backs out of the deal for a reason not contemplated in the contract will forfeit this sum. (We'll talk more about how that might play out in Chapter 10.) A buyer who goes through with the deal can either get a refund of the earnest-money deposit or, more likely, apply the money toward closing costs.

CAUTION

Be wary of accepting an offer from an overseas buyer until the earnest money deposit has cleared. With citizens of places like China and Russia having accumulated large amounts of cash in recent years, many are looking for places to park it. However, as many selling agents have found, actually getting that money out of certain countries can be difficult, and depend on an often-uncooperative government. "We've had to develop a policy of not going into contract with an overseas buyer unless the earnest money deposit has cleared," says Bellevue, Washington-based Realtor Patricia Wangsness. "I know of a house in our area that received multiple offers over asking, and the seller accepted the highest, from a non-U.S. buyer. But the house was back on the market seven days later, because the buyers couldn't come up with the earnest money. By then, several other buyers had lost interest and moved on. Ultimately, of course, there's also the question of whether non-U.S. buyers are able to transfer an even larger sum of cash for the down payment—but if they default at that point, you'll at least be able to keep the earnest money."

You may have specified an earnest-money requirement in your listing, and set the required amount, probably at a percentage of the purchase price. Sometimes this deposit is paid in two parts: a flat fee (typically $500 or $1,000) when the offer is submitted, and the rest, usually a percentage of the purchase price, when the contract is signed.

If you didn't request a specific amount, the buyer will make a choice depending on local custom (within any limits set by state law) and how badly the buyer wants the house. A high deposit indicates a high level of commitment to the deal.

By the way, you're not allowed to rush out and spend the money now. It's traditionally held by either your escrow or title company or your real estate agent.

Down Payment Amount

The offer should state how much the buyer plans to pay in cash toward the purchase price. Ideally, this amount will be 20% or more. Anything less than 5% makes the transaction risky, because the buyer may have a hard time finding a reputable institution to lend the rest (unless the buyer qualifies for a government-assisted loan).

The higher the down payment, the greater the chances that the buyer's loan will close successfully. The lender can feel comfortable that, in the event of a foreclosure, it will be able to sell the house for more than the amount still owed on the loan.

Look closely at exactly when the buyer plans to make the down payment. For example, the buyer may suggest putting down 10% within the first two weeks of signing the purchase agreement and the remaining 10% at closing. You can counteroffer with a request that the buyer make a larger down payment up front, as evidence of ability to perform.

Financing Contingency

A high offer amount is no good unless the buyer can really pull the entire sum of money together, most likely by getting a bank loan for everything above the down payment. This is hugely important to your deal going through.

Unless you receive an all-cash offer, the buyer will probably include a financing contingency in the language of the offer. This states that the agreement will be finalized only if the buyer applies for financing within a certain time period and then successfully obtains a loan on certain specified terms.

> **TIP**
>
> **All-cash offers are more common than you'd think.** About 15% of buyers paid all cash in 2013, according to NAR figures. An all-cash offer can be every seller's dream, as there's no need for the buyer to include a financing contingency. Such offers are particularly common from non-U.S. buyers, for whom your house may simply represent a safe way to invest their savings. However, due to the difficulties in money transfers from foreign countries described above, all-cash offers from non-U.S. buyers aren't as straightforward as they might first appear.

Buyers might state within the financing contingency, for example, that they'll accept only a fixed-rate loan at 4.5% interest or less—although not all offers are written to include this level of detail. If the buyer has been preapproved for the loan he or she wants, removing this contingency should not be a problem. But remember that the buyer's preapproval probably came with conditions, such as an appraisal. And the buyer needs to qualify for the loan right up to the closing day—a job loss or change in credit rating could undo this. Let's take a closer look at how to evaluate the financing contingency.

Make Sure the Buyer Has Been Preapproved by a Reputable Lender

Your first question should be about what efforts the buyer has already made to obtain financing. Any prepared buyer will have already gotten loan preapproval; that is, a lender's statement of willingness to lend a certain amount of cash. With preapproval for an amount equal to or greater than the sale price of your home, the buyer should be able to get the loan when the time comes.

Such preapproval is more important than ever, with lenders doing massive amounts of investigating and double-checking before giving actual, final approval to a loan—or else denying it.

> **CAUTION**
>
> **Even a preapproval isn't necessarily a commitment.** The most solid preapprovals are ones where the lender scrutinized the buyer's finances before preapproving, which is more likely to happen at established, reputable lending institutions rather than, say, a discount loan house.

Your real estate agent or attorney can help you evaluate which lenders are reputable. According to real estate agent Patricia Wangsness, "Our experience has led us to strongly prefer buyers who will be using a local lender. We had a situation where the couple buying our client's house had successfully used an online lender before, and wanted to use the same one again. But the lender sent an appraiser who was also from outside the area, and had no idea of local values. It was a $1.25 million house, but the appraiser said that figure was far too high—ignoring the value of the school system, the quality of the home builder, and the fact that (unlike the comparables), the house had a view. In our area, a view alone can add $50,000 to a home's value. We went out and paid for a second appraisal, which showed a value *above* what the home was being sold for. The deal eventually went through."

If the buyer hasn't been preapproved for a loan at all (or shown you a letter to prove it), your deal may be iffy. In the best-case scenario, the buyer may have started house shopping only recently, without realizing the need for loan preapproval. In the worst-case scenario, the buyer has bad credit and hasn't yet found a willing lender, but is hoping for a change of luck. In any case, take a look at the loan terms the buyer is hoping to get. If those seem completely out of whack in today's market, that's a strike against this offer. Also consider the buyer's down payment—the bigger it is, the more likely the buyer will get the needed financing, because the buyer's hefty investment lowers the lender's risk.

If you're inclined to continue with the negotiations with a buyer who isn't preapproved, insist that the buyer get preapproval from an established lender before you agree to include the financing contingency. Then ask your agent to call the lender and confirm the preapproval letter's authenticity. Also have the prospective buyer provide additional financial information, discussed below.

Selling a Condo?
Make Sure Lenders Won't Refuse to Touch It

If you're selling a condo, the buyers' eligibility isn't the lender's only concern. Under 2008 Fannie Mae/Freddie Mac guidelines, lenders must, before approving a condo loan, evaluate things like the condo association's financial stability, what percentage of the property is occupied by renters, how much space is reserved for certain usages, and more.

Not surprisingly, this has made it more difficult for buyers to take out loans for condo purchases. In markets where many existing structures have been converted to condos, the property may simply not fit the guidelines. One way you might deal with such potential problems is to get your condo property preapproved by a lender. In literal terms, you'd go to a mortgage broker and say, 'Can you find an investor that will lend on this condo?'

Once you have that preapproval, you can tell buyers that the condo has passed at least one lender's examination review and fits within the lending guidelines. You could even put a contingency into your purchase contract saying that the buyer must submit a loan application to that particular lender (among others, if the buyer wishes).

Make Sure the Buyer Is Seeking a Loan on Realistic Terms

The buyer may wish to gain protection from having to accept any old loan by specifying in the contract not only how much money he or she must succeed in borrowing (on one or more loans), but at what interest rate and with how many points, or other terms.

You can definitely require that the financing contingency be realistic. If the going interest rate is around 5%, and the buyer tries to condition the offer on getting a 4% loan, the buyer is unlikely to be able to meet that contingency. Insist on a change to the contract terms.

Set an Appropriate Schedule for the Buyer to Obtain Financing

Another issue to consider is when, in the weeks before the proposed deal would close, you'll find out about the likelihood that the buyer's financing will come through. The standard purchase contract mentions the date by which the buyer must submit a loan application (typically within a reasonable time period, such as five days). The contract should also state a date by which the lender must issue an actual loan commitment letter, which will itself contain certain conditions before final approval—perhaps verification of the buyer's employment or a professional appraisal of the house's value.

Make sure the date for this commitment letter isn't so far out that the buyer can withdraw from the transaction at the last minute, before the closing. For example, if the closing is scheduled for November 28, and the mortgage contingency date isn't until November 24, what happens if the buyer doesn't get the commitment? Your sale could fall apart—or more likely, you'll be asked for an extension of days or weeks.

Get Additional Financial Information From the Buyer

In today's tight credit market, you want as much financial information as possible from a potential buyer. For this reason, you might ask for additional documentation, to see for yourself whether the buyer is in a good position to get a mortgage loan.

Depending on the practice in your area, your agent may be able to request information from the buyer's agent. Some agents even create a questionnaire for the buyer to fill out. You're looking for details on things like the status of the mortgage approval, name and contact information for the lender and mortgage officer, where the down payment money will come from (such as cash on hand, pension, money market, gifts, or proceeds from another sale), whether the buyer must sell another property before buying yours, the buyers' credit scores, and so on.

Separate Appraisal Contingency

Sometimes included as part of the financing contingency, an appraisal contingency says that the buyer will close the deal only if the home's professionally appraised value is at least as much as the amount the buyer has contracted to pay for it. The appraisal contingency has become quite common due to changes in how banks must choose appraisers, says Massachusetts attorney Ken Goldstein: "The buyer may end up with an appraiser who, perhaps unfamiliar with the local market, appraises the house for less than its purchase price; or for even less than the loan amount. We're seeing many transactions fail for insufficient appraisals. While the buyer may be able to go back to the seller and get a lower purchase price, the buyer should also protect him- or herself by including an appraisal contingency."

Who Pays Which Fees

The buyer may ask for you to pay some fees (such as escrow fees, title search fees, deed preparation fees, notary fees, and transfer taxes), even if you haven't already volunteered to do so, by checking off boxes on a standard offer form or through some other written notation. Local practice often sets the norm for who pays what.

If you hadn't originally planned on paying these costs, don't reject them out of hand. They make a nice incentive for the buyer, which can be useful if you're trying to compensate for some part of your counteroffer that the buyer will be less happy about—for example, a rent-back period allowing you to stay in the home past the closing, or a shorter escrow period.

Evaluating Offer Contingencies and Terms

If the buyer's offer was written as a full contract (as is standard in some states), make sure that the other (nonfinancial) conditions and terms are acceptable to you. In some cases, especially if you receive two offers for the same amount, these terms—particularly certain "contingencies" that create easy escape hatches from your contract— may determine your final choice.

Closing Date

The closing date is when the transaction finalizes and the house is legally transferred from you to the buyer. Typically, the contract will specify an actual closing date, around 15 to 90 days into the future. In some states, however, standard contracts give a certain time window or say "on or before" or "on or after" a certain date.

If you are choosing among multiple offers, and the buyers sense that you want to move on to your next home quickly, some may schedule a quick closing, hoping to set their offer apart. Then again, some buyers (who will be doing most of the work in the days leading up to the closing and may have to sell their own home first) won't want to feel rushed into the purchase. Of course, you want to allow enough time for you and the buyer to do things right, and perhaps for you to find a new home and move out.

While the closing date shouldn't be the main thing that sways your decision for or against a certain offer, if you wait too long, not only will you delay your ability to get your money out of the house, but also the buyers may lose their financing if they have an expiration date on the lender's loan commitment or interest rate lock. So try to limit the closing date to no more than 60 days after the contract signing. And whatever you do, don't agree to close within a "reasonable time." What's reasonable to you may not be what's reasonable to the buyer. Far better to set a date, which you and the buyer can later agree (in writing) to change if you need to.

The contract may also state a separate date of possession. That's the day when the buyer can move into the property. Normally, this is the same date as the closing date, but you can agree on a different date.

Buyer's Sale of Other Property Contingency

A buyer who plans to sell another house before buying yours may not have any available cash until that sale happens. In fact, in 2013 the NAR reported that, with student loans, car loans, and other financial issues affecting prospective home buyers, especially the youngish ones, fewer and fewer buyers make down payments using savings. About one third of buyers must rely on proceeds from another house.

Such buyers may want a contingency in the purchase contract stating that the deal is conditional upon selling their own house first—that is, on actually closing escrow. (In Connecticut, they call this a "Hubbard clause.") Without such a contingency, the buyer could get stuck owing you for the house without having the means to pay for it.

Still, you're not going to be happy to see this contingency. In a hot market, where other would-be buyers are eager to step in, you can simply say "no" to this in your counteroffer, or move on to the next offer.

The contingency may, however, be a bit more palatable if the buyer's home is located in an area where sales are hot. Also look for assurances from the buyer's agent that they've been planning ahead and can literally put their house on the market tomorrow. Better yet, today.

If you agree to the buyer's-property-sale contingency, be sure to create a compromise that protects you: Ask that the contract include a "wipeout" or "kickout" clause, which lets you leave your house on the market while you wait for the buyer to sell. If you get another offer, you can advise the buyer, in essence, "You have xx hours (usually 72) to either wipe out the contingency and continue with the purchase or free me from the contract so I can sell to the other person." (Or you can accept the newest offer provisionally, as a backup offer, if you want to give the first buyer a little more time.)

If, after you invoke the wipeout clause, the buyer can't go forward with buying your house, the contract will be canceled. You'll have to return the earnest-money deposit, too. At that point, you'll be free to continue negotiations with the new offeror.

Inspection Contingency

Most buyers will want a chance to inspect your house and to either approve the results or negotiate over needed repairs, as a condition of finalizing the deal. An inspection contingency is, therefore, fairly standard.

Such a clause obviously leaves a giant window of opportunity for buyers who get cold feet and want to cancel the contract, however. No house is perfect. Most contracts provide that a defect must be "material" in order to justify the buyer canceling the deal, but with enough little flaws and dings, this threshold can easily be reached— and do you really want to sue someone over what's "material" in order to force them to buy your house?

Still, there's little reason to argue over a contingency that is standard and reasonable. If you've done your job and have fully disclosed issues with your property, the inspection shouldn't turn up any surprises—in which case it will be hard for the buyer to make an issue out of the inspector's findings.

If the market is super-hot, you may actually find a buyer who waives the inspection contingency. That would raise that offer higher in the pile in terms of likelihood of a successful closing—but don't look upon it as an opportunity to hide problems with the house. You will still need to provide the buyer with a complete set of written disclosures (which you may have already done by this point.)

Title Contingency

The buyer will also want the right to hire a title officer or attorney to review the history of your house's ownership, and time to obtain a title insurance policy. The basic idea of the title contingency is to make sure that you truly own the house outright, without any outstanding debts, liens, or encumbrances against it that won't be resolved by the time the transaction closes. This, too, is a reasonable term for buyers to put in the offer and contract.

Homeowners' Insurance Contingency

The buyer may wish to condition the sale on successfully obtaining homeowners' insurance coverage for your house. This probably isn't a contingency to fight about. First off, recognize that the buyer has no choice but to obtain homeowners' insurance—the lender will require it, and even in an all-cash purchase, the buyer would be foolish to go without it.

Making the sale contingent on getting the insurance protects the buyer if the property turns out to be uninsurable. The buyer might also ask you to provide a CLUE ("comprehensive loss underwriting") report. Drawn from an insurance industry database, it details the house's history of claims and damage awards. The more claims you've made, especially serious or water-related ones, the harder it will be for the next owner to get insurance.

Flood Zone Contingency

With flood insurance rates going up, buyers have become wary of buying houses that are in federally designated flood zones. Depending on your location, your buyer might add a contingency stating that he or she won't close until receiving a determination that the property is not in a flood zone.

At the very least, you should argue to adjust this contingency so that being in a flood zone alone is not enough to allow canceling the deal. This is because a flood-zone determination doesn't automatically mean that the lender will require the buyer to buy flood insurance. Try to condition the contract on a flood zone determination that actually requires the owner to buy insurance.

Attorney Review Contingency

The buyer may wish to put a clause in the final contract making the deal contingent on his or her attorney reviewing it. If the attorney is not satisfied with the results, you and the buyer would need to agree on the attorney's suggested modifications in order for the deal to go forward.

You won't need this review contingency if an attorney prepared the offer documents in the first place, as required by some states' laws. (New Jersey has a unique system in which the buyers and seller get three business days after signing a real-estate-agent-prepared purchase contract to terminate it based on an attorney's review. They may also negotiate to modify the agreement per their attorney's suggestions.)

You'd sign the contract with this contingency in place, but with the knowledge that the attorney may suggest amendments after the fact. This can be especially important for both buyer and seller if you're not using a real estate agent—in which case you should also include your own attorney review contingency.

Contingency for Review of Seller's Disclosure Report

In most states, buyers don't need to add this contingency—state law itself will condition the sale on you, the seller, filling out a form disclosing property conditions, defects, environmental hazards, and more, and on the buyer being satisfied with what's shown there before closing the sale.

But in a few states, no such laws exist, or they make an exception for certain properties such as condos. One way the buyer may seek protection in such a state is by asking you to provide written disclosures about the property's condition.

Contingency for Review of CC&Rs or Other Documents

If you're selling a condominium or other property in a common interest development, your buyer will no doubt request the right to review the CC&Rs, master deed, bylaws, rules and regulations, and other relevant documents before agreeing to the sale. The buyer's lender may also require these. These will reveal important things like how well-funded and well-run the governing association is, what the community rules are, and how much the buyer can expect to pay in homeowners' association fees and special assessments. It's only fair to agree to this contingency.

Neighbor Review Contingency

This is an example of a contingency that has developed by local custom, namely in Washington State. There, the homebuyer may request a three-day period in which to investigate things like the quality of local schools, how close the home is to bus lines and shopping, local noise levels, parking availability, and other environmental and safety conditions; and to cancel the deal if these aren't satisfactory.

The clause is unpopular among home sellers, because it gives buyers an easy out of the deal. There's something to complain about in every neighborhood! Unless the buyer's offer is the only one on the table, you might simply refuse to include that addition to the contract.

Final Walk-Through Contingency

Also called the buyer inspection, this allows the buyer to take a last look at the house, usually a day or two before the closing. The purpose is to make sure you have actually moved out, cleaned up, made any agreed-upon repairs, and left the place in good condition, with all fixtures intact. We'll talk about how to prepare for the walk-through in Chapter 10.

Other, Customized Contingencies

Although we've discussed the typical contingencies, others may be included in the standard offer form in your state, or you or the buyer can draft your own (with the help of an agent or attorney). (In Chapter 9 we'll talk more about contingencies you, as the seller, might want to add.)

The buyer is the one who is more likely to come up with unusual contingencies, based on details of your property or the circumstances of your sale. The buyer might, for example, want to make the offer contingent on verifying that zoning laws allow adding a second story. We've even heard of cases where buyers made offers after having viewed the house only through an online, virtual tour—then added a contingency giving them a chance to see, and like, the house in person.

Evaluating the Buyers' Agent

A scenario you want to avoid is one where you've taken the highest and otherwise best offer, only to spend the next six weeks going crazy because the buyers can't seem to get their financing together, they make ridiculous demands for repairs, or they find their own unique ways to be flaky or difficult.

You can't know the buyers' personalities in advance—but your agent (assuming he or she is experienced in the industry) will know, or know of, the agent who will be representing and speaking for them. A good buyers' agent won't let the buyers get away with difficult behavior, and will help educate and keep them on track when it comes to matters like financing and follow-through on removing contingencies. An inexperienced or unprofessional agent, on the other hand, may be tough to work with no matter the personalities or market experience of the buyers themselves.

As California Realtor Carol Neil puts it, "I have rejected offers, even if they were higher than others, because the buyer was rep-resented by an unrealistic or difficult agent. I imagine every other agent has, too."

Real estate agents come in all personalities and levels of profes-sionalism. You yourself may have a chance to compare their skills and personalities in a multiple-offer situation, where your agent schedules them for back-to-back offer presentations. Think twice about an offer where, for instance:

- the agent already gives indications of being a hardline negotia-tor, perhaps by asking for things that aren't traditional in your locale (for example, to have the seller, not the buyer, pay for escrow costs) or by peppering your agent with suspicious questions like, "What's that new drywall covering up?"

- the agent appears disorganized, shuffling papers around ("Gee, where did I put that letter from my clients?") and making you wonder whether he or she will really be able to close the deal without mishaps, or

- the agent insults your home in a misguided effort at negotiating, as in, "Of course, we would've offered more, but my clients need to set some money aside to rip out that overgrown weed patch and put in some real landscaping."

And you should rely on your agent's judgment on the buyer's agent's reputation in the community. Your agent and the buyer's agent may have worked together on many deals in the past. If it was an unpleasant experience—or worse yet, the buyer's agent's incompetence or obstreperous behavior led a deal to fall through—you can bet your agent will be telling you, "Look, I know it's the highest price, but here are some very good reasons why we don't want to work with these people." Heed this type of advice!

Back and Forth: From Offer to Contract

After a buyer has submitted an offer (or multiple buyers have done so), you can respond in one of three ways:

- Accept the offer.
- Reject the offer.
- Make a counteroffer.

Accepting the Offer

If you receive an offer that you like and it's already in the form of a proposed contract, you are happy with the price, the buyer's finances line up, and everything else looks good, you don't have much more to do. (This doesn't happen very often!) You'd need only to sign the offer document and return it to the buyer—you'd then have a contract that binds both of you (subject to getting it reviewed by an attorney, if that's required in your state or included as a contingency in your contract).

CAUTION
You may be legally obligated to accept an offer—but only if it's perfect. In a few states, if a buyer comes in with a totally clean, no-contingency, full-price offer, you must either sell to that person or take the house off the market.

If the buyer presents the offer orally or as a short document and you want to accept it, you can let the buyer know and then figure out the logistics of drafting a contract (most likely, through each of your agents or attorneys working together). You and the buyer will then negotiate over the contract until you've got it into a form that both of you are happy to sign.

Until that contract is signed, however, neither of you is bound by the agreement, which means either one of you could walk away. For that reason, some buyers ask for what's called a binder, which is a preliminary agreement secured by the buyer's payment of earnest money (usually a nominal amount). Think of it as a contract to negotiate a contract. Binders can be helpful in situations where, for instance, the attorneys can't get together right away, and the buyer wants assurances that another buyer won't step in. However, for ordinary situations, many attorneys counsel against binders. Richard Leshnower, an attorney in New York, explains: "A binder is often more trouble than it's worth. Because it's not a full purchase contract, there are a lot of terms it doesn't have, and you can end up with messy and expensive litigation between two parties who are, realistically, never going to agree to the sale." It's probably simpler and more straightforward to focus your energies on getting an agreement on paper with which both you and the buyer are comfortable.

Rejecting the Offer

Maybe you can already tell—perhaps by an absurdly low price or an unrealistic contingency—that a particular buyer's offer is so far from what you're looking for that you will do nothing but waste your time and delay your eventual sale if you try to counteroffer or negotiate. If so, your agent can contact the buyer's agent with the bad news.

TIP

Have the courtesy to respond. Some sellers do nothing when they receive an offer they don't plan to accept or negotiate. Better to have your agent make the call, and even briefly describe the problem ("The offer was so far below the asking price that we really didn't think it would be possible to find a middle ground"). The buyers may even respond by correcting the problem.

Another possibility, if you don't have better offers coming in, is to counteroffer, as described next. Maybe the buyers weren't really making the strongest offer they were capable of, and will come up in price and drop or adjust some of the contingencies.

Making a Counteroffer

There are so many different terms in an offer that it's rare to receive one that meets your criteria in every respect. If an offer looks promising, but you'd prefer a few changes or additions, you can counteroffer.

Counteroffers are a normal part of nearly every real estate deal. You might suggest a higher price than was offered (but probably lower than your list price, if you want negotiations to go anywhere). Or you might add terms of your own, for example by responding to a tight closing date with a clause allowing you to rent back the house for a couple of weeks.

TIP

You don't have to counter the highest offer. If a lower-priced offer comes in with many attractive features—perhaps the buyers are in great shape financially, and their agent is highly experienced and easy to work with—then you can counter that offer before responding to the others. Your two agents might talk informally first, about whether it's worth giving the buyers an opportunity to step to the front of the line.

If you end up accepting a lower-than-list-price offer, and it includes an inspection contingency, consider counteroffering with a request for dollar limits on any repair needs that come up post-inspection. For example, if you've listed your house for $350,000 but decide to accept $320,000, you probably don't want to be nickeled and dimed over repairs. You might limit repair costs to, say, $5,000 or $6,000. (In some states, such a limit is written into the standard contract, although you're free to change the amount.)

Arranging for Backup Offers

Choosing among multiple offers can feel like you're putting all your eggs in one basket. If the deal you select falls through, other prospective buyers whose offers were also quite attractive may be long since gone.

One possible way to protect yourself is to ask your second-choice offeror to leave the offer open, as a "backup offer." Then, if the chosen deal falls apart, you can accept the backup. Or, if the first offeror is asking for a lot of concessions, you can use the backup offer as negotiating leverage. Unfortunately, the buyer in the backup position can withdraw the offer at any time, and may also condition the backup position on your giving a final acceptance or rejection within a limited time, perhaps only a few days. On top of that, if your first-choice buyer knows about the backup deal (information that the agents might share), he or she may feel like you're playing the field a bit too much, making for a rocky start to your relationship.

A less formal, but often more effective approach is to call the agent for the second-choice buyer and say, "We appreciate your offer, but we expect to move forward on another one. If anything happens, however, we'll get in touch." That helps keep your house in the minds of the alternate buyers and their agent.

The form of your counteroffer depends on local custom and what form the original offer took. If the original offer would have worked as a stand-alone contract, you might (as in California) need to start from scratch and fill out a whole new version of the exact same form. Or you might create a simpler document, essentially saying, "I agree to the terms of the offer, but with these changes." Simpler still, you and your agent might suggest a counteroffer verbally during your initial meeting with the buyer's agent, and the buyer's agent might call the buyer to discuss the matter before the final step, when it all gets put into writing (and only then becomes legally binding).

If your counteroffer terms are acceptable, the buyer may either sign on and create a contract or submit further counteroffers. This process may go back and forth until you've come to an agreement that either is or can be formalized in a written document. (But be sure to put expiration dates on your counteroffers, in case the buyer sits back and does nothing.)

Signing the Purchase Contract

Once you've agreed on the terms of your sale, there's one last important step: signing off on the document that becomes your purchase agreement. By now, one of you has probably either created an offer or counteroffer that will serve as a final contract, or you've come to a close enough agreement that it will be easy for either your real estate agent or attorney to put it in written form. Before signing, however, give the contract one last read-through. The next chapter will help you do this. ●

Demystifying Your House Sale Contract

Once you've agreed on the terms of your house sale, there's one last important step: signing off on the document that becomes your purchase agreement. Hopefully by now you or the buyer has created an offer or counteroffer that will serve as a final contract, or you've come to a close enough agreement that it will be easy for your real estate agent or attorney to put it in written form. But if not, this chapter will help you settle on those terms, and alert you to some important ones that you may want to add. Either way, before you sign, give the contract one last read-through, to make sure you understand all the terms to which you're agreeing.

At the end of the contract negotiations, you (and any co-owners of your house) will simply sign and date the latest version of the contract. The buyers will need to sign, too. Or, if they've already signed but you've mutually agreed to certain changes, they may need to initial the changes. The buyer's real estate agent may also need to sign, essentially as a witness to the buyer's signature.

Only when you have a written document, signed by both you and the buyer, are you legally bound by your agreement. Even if you've engaged in long negotiations and gotten many verbal assurances, without a signed contract, you have nothing to fall back on if the buyer changes his or her mind.

What You Should—Or Shouldn't— See in Your Purchase Contract

Let's run through the contract clauses you're likely to encounter. While the standard contract varies by state, the basics tend to be fairly uniform. And if you've read the previous chapter, you're already familiar with many of the meatier concepts, such as the typical real estate contract contingencies.

When in doubt, ask your real estate agent or attorney to decode the contract language—whichever of them prepared or reviewed it for you.

- **Parties.** The names of the buyer and seller.

- **Property description.** At a minimum, the address and a physical description (such as "a single-family home"), with a few details as to what the property includes, such as a garage. In some states (such as New York), the contract will refer to a separate attachment containing a legal description of the property— that is, a metes and bounds word description of the land being conveyed. A survey may also be included.
- **Expiration date.** The time limit for you to accept (or counteroffer) the buyer's offer.
- **Offer or purchase amount.** The price the buyer intends to pay (subject to further negotiations before the closing).
- **Earnest money amount.** The amount the buyer will give to your agent or escrow holder upon or soon after signing the agreement. The buyer agrees to forfeit this money to you, the seller, if the buyer backs out for a reason not allowed for within the contract. The amount of the deposit will vary depending on location; it's usually from 1% to 10% of the purchase amount, subject to any maximum set by state law.
- **Down payment amount.** How much the buyer will pay in cash toward the purchase price.
- **Contingencies.** Conditions that must be met by both the buyer and seller before the deal closes (the house is actually sold). For example, the buyer might reasonably ask for an inspection contingency and a financing contingency, and you might include a contingency allowing you to remain in the home beyond the closing date (in order to have time to find or move to your next home). We discussed the buyer's contingencies in depth in Chapter 8, and will talk more about possible seller contingencies below. When reviewing contingencies, make sure the contract allows for a reasonable time for each to be dealt with and removed—but doesn't leave you in suspense until near to the closing date.
- **Title.** You'll need to promise that you're in a legal position to sell the property, without any debts or other liens or encumbrances that interfere with its marketability. The process

of the buyer obtaining title insurance will help confirm and resolve any such issues. For example, the title search sometimes turns up tax or child support liens that the seller must pay off before the sale goes forward. The property may have some encumbrances, too, either in writing (such as a utility company having an "easement" to run a gas line under the property) or that have been created over time (such as the public's right to cross a corner of the property as a shortcut). So long as such encumbrances are made known to the buyer as part of the contracting process or covered by the buyer's title insurance policy, they shouldn't be a problem; but some may require a lawyer's help, as discussed in Chapter 2.

- **Seller representations.** You may have to make certain assurances about the property, for example, that to your knowledge, the roof is free of defects or, in a condo or co-op, that you know of no mold or pest problems in the building where your unit is located.

- **Fixtures and personal property.** Fixtures (items permanently attached to the property, like built-in appliances or fences) normally stay with the house unless you and the buyer agree and specify otherwise, while personal property goes with you, unless you and the buyer agree otherwise. The contract boilerplate may list examples of fixtures, such as built-in appliances, screens, storm windows, Venetian blinds, drapery hardware, cabinet knobs, awnings, antennas, plants, and fences. But you can modify these if the buyer agrees. Some buyers may also want to buy some nonfixtures (personal property) within the house such as an entry rug or mirror that's perfect for its location, your riding mower, or something else. This is an area where you and the buyer both need to be attentive to the possibility of misunderstanding. In some states, for example, it's customary to leave all major appliances (refrigerator, dishwasher, and so on) behind, while in other states it's not. The same goes for curtains.

CAUTION

Flat-screen TVs are an item of frequent contention. When mounted on the wall, complete with brackets and wires running through drilled holes, flat-screen televisions look like the classic fixture. (That wall is going to look ugly when the TV is gone.) Nevertheless, TVs have a long history of being considered personal property in the real estate industry. So if you've got a flat-screen, be sure the buyers are clear on whether or not you will leave it behind. You may, if you're willing to part with it, be able to sell it to them.

- **Rights of use.** If you're selling a condo, co-op, or townhouse, you may be transferring to the buyer your right to use portions of the property that you either don't own yourself or that you own jointly with others, such as a specific parking space. The contract should make this clear.

- **Prorations and assessments.** How you and the buyer will split recent and upcoming fees like mortgage interest, property taxes, and homeowners' association fees. If the contract says "as of the date of possession," and that date falls on a Wednesday, for example, you would have to pay expenses through Tuesday and the buyer would pay them from Wednesday onward.

- **Closing agent (or "escrow holder").** This is the person or company who will act as an intermediary, assisting with pre-closing tasks and holding onto any money that you or the buyer deposit in advance. This may be a title company, escrow company, or attorney. The choice of closing agent isn't usually something you need to argue over. If the buyer has already named a reputable company within the draft contract, it's probably fine to use that company.

- **Fees.** A list of the fees to be paid before and during the closing—including escrow fees, title search fees, deed preparation fees, notary fees, transfer taxes, and so on—and who will pay them. Local custom usually dictates who is responsible for the various transactional fees. You might consider paying some of these, even if you hadn't originally planned to, in order to compensate for an aspect of your counteroffer that the buyer isn't happy about—for example, a rent-back period for you or a shorter escrow period.

- **Closing date.** The date the transaction finalizes and the house legally belongs to the buyer. Typically, the contract will specify an actual closing date, around 15 to 90 days into the future. In some states, however, standard contracts give a certain time window or say "on or before" or "on or after" a certain date. (Usually these end up being a window of approximately 30 days.) Try to limit the closing date to no more than 60 days after the contract signing. Don't agree to open-ended language, such as a closing within a "reasonable time."

- **Possession.** The date the buyer can actually possess (move into) the property. This is normally the closing date or one day after. Although you can ask to retain possession for a longer time (likely by paying rent), the buyer's lender may demand that the buyer take possession within 30 days of the closing.

TIP

Avoid closing on a Friday. By real estate tradition, closings are often scheduled for a Friday toward the end of the month. But a paperwork snafu could easily result in the delay of your closing by one business day. That puts everyone in limbo for the entire weekend. Better to ask that the closing be set for a Wednesday or Thursday.

- **Agent payment or commissions.** What payment will be made to the real estate agents representing you and the buyer. (See Chapter 2 for a discussion of agent commissions, which you, the seller, usually pay in full from the proceeds of the sale.)

- **Risks of loss or damage to property.** How damage to the property (such as from a fire) during escrow will affect the agreement. Usually, any such losses are the sellers' to deal with (see Chapter 10 for more on this).

- **Resolving disputes.** How you and the buyer will resolve any legal disputes, and whether you'll use alternative resolution methods before going to court (such as mediation or arbitration).

To avoid the prospect of litigation, agreeing to one of these alternative dispute resolution methods is standard.

- **Entire agreement.** A statement that you and the buyer don't have any other agreement between you and that if you want to alter the one you have, you'll do it in writing and you'll both sign it. Remember, side agreements regarding what personal property stays or goes with the house are not enforceable. So if the buyer assured you that, for example, it's fine for you to take your old Wedgewood stove (which would normally be considered a "fixture" that stays with the property), be sure to get this written into the agreement.

- **Time is of the essence.** This confirms that if a date was important enough for you to write into the agreement—for example, the closing date—it's a fundamental part of it, and if either you or the buyer don't make the date (or modify the agreement), then you'll have breached the contract.

- **Signatures.** No matter who goes first, you don't have a contract until both of you have signed.

Your agent or attorney can tell you about special contract requirements in your state. Your contract may also include other terms—for example, it may address an existing lease if the property is being rented to a tenant or may specify how all documents must be transmitted (in person or electronically).

Adding Your Own Contract Terms and Contingencies

When we discussed the various contingencies that the buyer might put in the purchase offer (in Chapter 8), we were assuming the buyer wouldn't have a rush of empathy and include contingencies that benefit you. In fact, there's probably not much that you want to ask for as a contingency of the sale—your main interest, after all, is in seeing the deal go through, not in finding a means of escape from it. Nevertheless, there are a couple terms and contingencies that are not uncommon for sellers to ask for.

Seller's Purchase of Other Property Contingency

If you haven't found a new abode yet, you may want to protect yourself from the possibility of having to find temporary digs after the sale of your house. One way to do that is with a contingency stating that the closing won't happen until you either sign an agreement to buy a replacement home or actually close on that purchase. (If you're planning to rent rather than buy, you can alternatively add a contingency related to your signing a lease.)

The buyer is not going to like this clause. If the market is hot enough, however, and you can easily find another buyer, your current buyer doesn't have much negotiating power. Still, any smart buyer will seriously balk at leaving this clause too open-ended. Expect to negotiate a reasonable amount of time, perhaps up to three weeks, to sign a purchase agreement for your next home (good luck getting any buyer to wait until you actually close the deal).

If the buyer does accept this contingency, he or she may rightfully insist on longer-than-usual periods of time in which to remove other contingencies, such as for inspections and financing. Why should the buyer pay to get all his or her ducks in a row, after all, when you may cancel the sale at the last minute?

When preparing this clause it's important to make clear who's actually responsible for declaring the contract canceled. Do you need to step forth and do so, or is that the buyer's role? It's in your interest to leave this to the buyer. In fact, you can draft the contract so that until the buyer actually cancels the contract based on your failure to remove the contingency, you can still come forward and say, "I did it, we're in contract to buy," and your home sale will continue moving forward. (This is how the standard California contract deals with it.)

We'll talk more in Chapter 10 about how to proceed with this contingency. Needless to say, you will need to act quickly.

If the buyer refuses to agree to this contingency altogether, your next best option is to ask for a longer closing period.

Seller Rent-Back After the Closing

If you think you'll need a little extra time in which to move after the sale closes—or are just reluctant to leave your home until you're certain the buyer will, in fact, close the deal—one possibility is to arrange for what's called a "rent-back." You literally become a tenant in your own home. The new owner becomes your landlord as soon as the house sale closes.

Such an agreement should allow you to stay in the home for a specific amount of time in exchange for daily or monthly rent, depending on the length of time you will remain there. In a hot market, however, an eager buyer may allow you to live in the house for a month or more rent-free.

Best thing we ever did **Negotiate for a long rent-back.** "When we put our house on the market, we weren't sure how much it would sell for," says Kathleen, "so we didn't know what we'd be able to afford next. But with two small children (ages five and two), the prospect of spending time and money finding and renting an apartment in between homes (tricky, without signing a six-month lease), not to mention storing all of our stuff and then essentially moving twice, seemed like a nightmare. Fortunately, we received competing offers. We were able to make a rent-back a big part of our counteroffer. The buyer we chose was willing to let us stay for three months, which allowed us to find a house, close the deal, and move, all before the rent-back ended."

According to Texas Realtor Greg Nino, "Seller rent-backs are included in nearly all the home sales I'm involved with right now. Some sellers don't want to drive their U-Hauls to the closing, not to mention worry that it won't happen that day! It's nice for them to be able to attend the closing, head back home, and wrap things up for the next four or five days. Besides, the seller may be depending on the closing to bring in the proceeds that will allow them to close on their next home. Rent-backs have actually become so common that if I'm representing the buyer, and the seller doesn't ask for a rent-back, I get worried, wondering if the listing agent forgot to ask, and is going to come begging for one a week before closing."

To arrange the rent-back, you will not only need to include this term in the purchase contract, but prepare a separate lease that you both sign. The lease should specify terms such as:

- the rent per week or month (high enough to cover your new landlord's mortgage, insurance, taxes, utilities, and other carrying costs, and maybe more, to compensate for the inconvenience of a delayed move)
- the lease term (your departure can be either a specific date or be left open ended, but the buyer will need to run this arrangement past its lender, because some lenders won't allow a rent-back that lasts more than 60 days, if it allows them at all), and
- who pays for utilities and for any damage that occurs while you're renting back (in theory, the buyer is responsible for property upkeep, but if you cause damage while you live there, the buyer will understandably want you to pay up).

If the buyers agree to a rent-back, do your best to remember that after the closing, they view the house as theirs, and may be suspicious of how you're treating it. You, meanwhile, might understandably still feel like the house is yours. The written agreement will help to keep this arrangement professional and businesslike.

Attorney Review Contingency

You may wish to put a clause in your final contract making the deal contingent on your own attorney reviewing it and being satisfied with the results. (As discussed in Chapter 8, the buyer may have already asked for such a contingency.)

Attorney preparation or review of the real estate contract is required in some states. The attorney may suggest amendments even after the contract has been signed. ●

Keeping Up Momentum, From Escrow to Closing

Once the contract has been signed and escrow opened, many people will spring into action: The escrow or title agent will start ordering or preparing title reports, preparing the property deed, and more; the buyer's lender will begin in-depth review and processing of the loan and order a professional appraisal of your home; and the buyer will arrange for pest and general inspections, line up homeowners' insurance, plus work on meeting any other contingencies.

Thankfully, your responsibilities during this time period are relatively few. (Good thing, since you'll be plenty busy either looking for a home to buy or planning your move and disposing of possessions, if you haven't already moved.)

Your most important tasks relative to the escrow process will include making your home available for inspections and appraisals, preparing various forms and statements (such as disclosures if you haven't already prepared these, and any other forms required locally, such as a smoke detector certificate), and meeting any other legal obligations or contingencies you agreed to in your contract, within the promised time frame. For example, you may need to get copies of permits for remodeling work you did on your kitchen, or you may need to add smoke or carbon monoxide detectors to comply with your state's law.

More generally, you'll need to be available and responsive when issues arise. If the title search turns up, for instance, a lien on your property placed by a contractor who claims you didn't pay the bill, you'll need to deal with this to clear the property's title. If the inspection uncovers repair needs, you'll have to decide how to respond to the buyer's requests, which might include consulting with contractors or making actual repairs.

Plan on staying in close touch with your real estate and escrow agents (and attorney, if you're using one) during this time, to make sure you stay on track. There's always a risk that the buyer will have a change of mind about the purchase—and you wouldn't want to make matters worse by missing a deadline or forgetting to respond to a request.

Taking Care of the House During Escrow

Even though you're in contract to sell, and may have moved out, your house is still yours to care for. That means making sure your insurance policy remains in force, continuing to pay your mortgage, keeping the lights, water, and utilities on, and if you've moved out, otherwise keeping an eye on the place.

Paying Your Mortgage on Time

The fact that you must continue making your mortgage payments as scheduled should go without saying. Nevertheless, sellers have been known to simply stop these payments as soon as they were in escrow. They've rightly figured out that the bank won't be able to foreclose before the sale closes. What they've forgotten is that the bank will assess penalties and interest, which the seller must then pay at closing. Oops.

Updating Your Insurance Coverage

If you're still living in the home, and are current on your homeowners' insurance payments, your coverage shouldn't be an issue. But if you've already moved out, your vacancy may trigger (usually after 30 or 60 days) a provision in your policy that allows your insurer to deny coverage in the event of damage or simply cancel the entire policy. Insurance companies include these provisions in order to protect themselves against the risks presented by vacant homes, which are unattended to and may attract thieves, vandals, or even teens looking for a place to hold a party. (The latter situation might create financial liability for personal injuries as well as property damage.)

According to Texas RE/MAX Realtor Greg Nino, "I've seen situations where pipes burst during the escrow period, or where someone broke into the empty house and stole all the copper pipes. Water everywhere, and no coverage, because the home seller had failed to advise the insurance company that he was going to vacate."

Review your policy to see if it has such a provision—look for words like "vacancy," "abandonment," or "neglect." If it does, you have two options to avoid trouble. Either get in touch with your insurance company or take steps to show that you're staying in the house at least a few times per week. If you opt for the latter approach, be sure to install enough furniture and amenities in the house to show that you really live there. (Yes, the adjuster may visit the house if you call and make a claim.) One definition of "vacancy" used by insurers is that the house does not have enough furniture and conveniences for basic habitability. At the very least, put in a mattress, pillow, and lamp!

The safer approach is to contact your insurance company and explain the situation. Your insurer can likely sell you either an endorsement to your existing policy (which shouldn't cost more than around $100) or a separate "vacant-home" policy. Or, you may need to turn to a separate insurance company for the vacant-home policy.

Keeping an Eye on the House After You've Moved

Even if your house is well insured, it's worth taking sensible measures to avoid it becoming a target for the aforementioned thieves, vandals, and partying kids. Many of these are similar to steps you take to protect your home when you go on vacation.

Don't expect your agent to take on these tasks. As Patricia Wangsness (a Coldwell Banker agent in Bellevue, Washington) says, "Our responsibility is to get the house sold, but we're not going to be able to check on it every night."

If you don't already have a security system or smoke detectors connected to a central monitoring service, now might be a good time to install them. (These can be pricey, but there's a lot at stake here, even if you are insured.) Some real estate agents actually offer their clients temporary alarm systems, with portable equipment and a month-to-month monitoring contract.

Best thing we ever did **Visit my house every morning during escrow.** "I was lucky enough to have moved a mere two miles away from the house I was selling," explains Anjali. "So I'd head back every morning, mostly to turn on the fountain. Thank goodness I did—I'd find something to deal with nearly every morning, whether it was a huge broken branch in the back yard after a windstorm, pizza containers that local high-schoolers left in the front yard, flyers hanging on the front door handle, or rotting lemons in the bowl that the stager had set out."

Besides trying to keep an eye on the house yourself, it's worth asking your neighbors to watch for problems or suspicious activity, and to pick up any stray packages or flyers they see on your front porch. Forward your mail and newspapers, if you haven't already. Put your lights on timers or (in the case of outdoor lights) sunlight sensors. Chances are these various measures won't stop a crime in progress, but you might prevent one by making your presence felt or at least minimizing the signs of your absence.

What about keeping the place looking nice? Now isn't a good time to fire your gardeners, swimming pool company, snow removal service, and so on. Poor maintenance is another clue that the home is unoccupied. Besides, anything could happen to your current deal, and the house is still, in theory, on the market until it's sold. Also, if you live in a community run by a homeowners' association (HOA) its regulations might require that lawns be mowed regularly, gardens be irrigated to prevent brown lawns or dried-up plants, and other maintenance be attended to.

Keeping the Lights and Utilities On

Here's another common mistake made by sellers who've moved out of the house: canceling lights, water, garbage, and other services. First off, this isn't nice to the buyer, because it's typically easier to transfer services than to restart them.

But canceling such services is not going to do you any good, either. When the home inspector arrives, and then later when the buyers do their final walk-through, they won't be able to see their way around or check whether the faucets, heating system, and so forth are in working order. They're likely to demand that you restore services before they release the relevant contingencies.

Check in with the buyer (through your agents) about two weeks before you'd like your services canceled, so that the buyer can request a transfer at the appropriate time. Alternatively, the buyer may ask you to agree to pay for the original services to continue after the closing, typically for 48 hours.

Notifying Your Homeowners' Association If Leaving the Home Vacant

If you live in a condo, townhome, or other house in a common interest development (CID), you may have obligations under your CC&Rs or other rules and regulations that apply during your escrow period. Check your governing documents to find out.

You will certainly need to keep paying your dues and assessments. It's also likely that you will need to notify the HOA of any dates that you may be leaving your house unoccupied. Even if not required, it's a good idea to give your HOA a heads-up. It might inform (or require you to inform) the community manager or security personnel (if your development employs security guards) of your vacancy. If the CID does employ security guards, find out whether they can conduct periodic checks on your house after you've moved and before the closing.

Getting Past the Appraisal Contingency

Even though you've found a buyer willing to purchase your house for a price you're willing to sell it for—or maybe, if a bidding war occurred, for a price that had you screaming with delight—that's not always the end of the discussion. Except in the rare case when a buyer is paying all cash for your home, the buyer's mortgage lender will no doubt require that the property be appraised. That means that a professional, selected by the lender, will come to your house and look around, then place a dollar value on it. If the appraisal comes in lower than the contract price, the bank will not approve the buyer's loan, and if there's an appraisal or financing contingency in your contract, that could kill the deal.

It used to be that appraisals were little more than formalities, which lenders conducted in order to make sure that buyers weren't purchasing tear-down trash heaps. Because of rapid home appreciation, appraisers tended to sign off on whatever price the buyer put forth. Not so today, with lenders edgy after having recently lost money to defaulting homeowners and gotten stuck with properties worth less than the mortgages held against them. Basically, the lender has to make sure it can, in the event of a foreclosure, sell the property for at least the amount it's lending to the buyer.

You can't actually influence the appraiser's judgment of your house's value, though it doesn't hurt to make sure the house looks good and that you've resolved any obvious repair or safety issues before the appraiser comes over and looks around. What you can do, however, is make sure the appraiser has all the information necessary to set an appropriate value for your home.

According to Washington Realtor Patricia Wangsness, "As listing agents, we always meet the appraiser with a comparative market analysis in hand. Some are more open to this than others. We're not interfering with the process, but it's a way to try and educate them on the local market. Besides, some of them do so-called 'drive-by' appraisals, which don't take much of anything into account. As agents, we're also allowed to ask whether an appraiser is familiar with the area—and we do ask. If we discover that, for example, an appraiser sent from the Olympic Peninsula is attempting to set a value on a downtown Seattle condo, we work extra hard to get them the appropriate market information." Ask your selling agent what his or her approach to interacting with the home appraiser is.

What should you and the buyer do if, after efforts such as these, the appraisal comes in low? The buyer may be equally outraged at the result, and perhaps be willing to dispute the stated appraisal value with the bank. Or, the buyer may come up with extra cash to augment the down payment and thus reduce the loan amount. If those strategies don't work, the buyer may look elsewhere for a loan.

If none of the above steps succeed, you're going to have to decide whether to accept a lower price for the home—possibly its appraised value minus the down payment, which is the maximum the lender will allow the buyer to pay. That may be the maximum the buyer will be *willing* to pay, too, after hearing a professional's take on what the house is really worth—or the buyer may start to get a little greedy, figuring that you're more likely to continue the deal with him or her than to put the house back on the market.

Dealing With the Inspection Contingency

Another hurdle to clear is the inspection contingency. Hopefully, your own advance inspection of the property has ruled out major problems that can't be fixed (such as pervasive mold) or ones that significantly reduce the property's value (such as foundation or roof trouble, or remodeling that wasn't up to code). But even if your home is free of major red flags, it's practically guaranteed to have a few defects.

As Massachusetts Realtor Nancy Atwood says, "All homes (except new construction) have issues that we refer to as the 'price of homeownership': loose tiles, old paint, and so forth." And the buyer's inspector wouldn't be doing the job right without noting everything in the report from a missing cover plate on an electrical outlet to a crack in the foundation.

> **TIP**
>
> **The inspection report isn't a repair list.** Some sellers are under the misapprehension that they must fix every defect listed on the inspection report. That's far from the case—though these do become matters for negotiation, as described next.

Your contract probably gives the buyer a certain number of days (such as three) within which to "approve" or "disapprove" the inspection report. It matters very little how bad the problems are—while buyers are theoretically only allowed to run away over "material" defects, getting lawyers involved to argue over whether the defects are truly "material" would probably cause more delay than would simply cancelling the deal and finding a new buyer. (Okay, you can fight to keep the earnest money if you really want to, but this too could be a fruitless effort—the escrow company is not a lawyer, and won't step in to decide who's right or wrong. So you're back to paying lawyer fees, which will quickly eat into the amount at stake.) The bottom line is that the buyer now has an opportunity to say, "Forget it," and end the deal.

Most buyers don't, however, cut and run. More likely, the buyer will negotiate over the needed repairs. How hard the buyer negotiates depends on the market. In a hot market, the buyer will likely let many or most repairs slide—though if the inspection turns up a major issue, such as a foundation that needs $50,000 worth of work, a buyer who's already bid top dollar for your home may ask for repairs or money back. This is especially true because the buyer knows that you're now duty-bound to disclose this newly discovered defect to all subsequent potential purchasers, thus lowering your house's value accordingly. You can try holding firm, but will have to make a strategic decision about how much you want to risk the buyer saying, "No thanks."

Best thing we ever did

Cancel the contract with an unwilling home buyer. According to Samuel, "Our home sale seemed to be going smoothly until the inspections. The buyers, a married couple, made a fuss over every little thing, demanding repair after repair. Finally I got frustrated, refused to make further concessions, and the deal was over. Later, I discovered that the husband and wife disagreed over whether they really wanted the home. It was the husband who was making all the trouble. I'm glad I didn't drag matters out further, because looking back, it was clear that they were never going to close on the purchase."

If the market remains cool in your area, or the buyer is simply a difficult personality or has cold feet, it's possible the buyer will haggle over every little repair.

If you agree to compensate the buyer for some of the defects that turned up in the inspection report, you can arrange for this in one of the following ways:

- **An escrow credit.** Instead of getting the full price at closing, you can agree to have the amount needed for repairs transferred directly to the buyer at closing or put into an escrow account (maintained by your escrow or title agent). The buyer can draw on the escrow account any time after the closing. But this can get tricky; a very stringent lender won't fund the loan until the repairs are made, thus delaying the closing. To circumvent this, many real estate experts recommend describing the credit as for "closing costs" rather than for "repairs," to avoid calling the lender's attention to it. To set an appropriate amount for the credit, you'll probably need to get bids from contractors.

- **A reduction in the sale price.** If your house is worth less than originally thought as a result of the defects, you can also just lower the price to reflect that. This lowers any required transfer taxes (for whoever has to pay them) as well as the buyer's annual property tax. Your agent may not like this option, because it also lowers your commission payment. Of course, figuring out how much to lower the price by is tricky—again, you might want to get bids for repairs.

- **Repairs to be made by you.** It's unlikely, but possible, that the buyer will ask you to make repairs. (Most buyers prefer to be in charge of overseeing repairs themselves.) While you have to come up with cash if the buyer requests this, at least you'll be able to choose the contractor and have some control over the price—or if it's a simple fix-up, you could even take care of it yourself.

Lesson learned the hard way **Understand and oversee those repairs carefully.** According to Nell, "The buyers' offer for my mother's house was contingent on us doing some repair work on the heating vents, but the details were fairly vague. We hired someone who didn't do the work properly, which we didn't find out until the buyers' final inspection, two days before the closing. To avoid having the deal fall through, we credited the buyers several thousand dollars. Had we hired a more competent contractor, and figured out exactly what work the buyers wanted done, we could have saved a lot of last-minute anxiety, and probably spent less overall."

- **Buyer arranges for repairs before closing and you pay the bill.** This should be the buyer's last choice—and yours as well. It requires three-way coordination between you, the buyer, and the buyer's repair people while you're still potentially living in the house, as well as dealing with the possibility that the repairs will take longer than expected.

When the Deal Depends on You Buying Another Home

If you included a clause in your purchase contract stating that the deal won't close until you've found—and most likely signed a purchase agreement to buy—your next home, you've hopefully already begun your home search. You may have mere days in which to get a contract signed with the seller of your next home—and as you now know, counteroffers can fly back and forth for days before a contract is actually signed.

If your buyer was willing to sign onto this clause in the first place, he or she is probably either ready to be patient or really, really wants your house. But that patience may eventually run out. You might want to work on a backup plan in case you can't find a house to buy in time.

If you can't meet the time limitations set forth in the contract, you can try to negotiate for an extension or (depending on the way your contract is written) ask that your buyer simply hold off on canceling the deal. The buyer will appreciate hearing about your good faith efforts to find a house or that you're almost in contract with a seller.

TIP

Don't be hasty in removing your home purchase contingency. Let's say you've successfully signed an agreement to buy your next house, but still have a few days before your sale contract requires you to remove this contingency. It might be wise to take that time to get your inspections done on your next home—a common stage when deals fall through.

Dealing With the Title Contingency

If any clouds on your house title are discovered, you'll need to deal with them quickly—which can sometimes mean coming up with some immediate cash. For example, if there's a lien on your house for unpaid child support, it's probably not going to be removed until you pay the child support. If your back fence is encroaching on the neighbor's property, you may need to have it moved.

Preparing for the Buyer's Final Walk-Through

Another, often overlooked, contingency that's probably in your contract is the final walk-through. This allows the buyer and buyer's agent, as one of the last steps during the days or hours before the closing, to visit your house and make sure that you've left it in the physical condition that you promised. You'll need to have moved out of the house completely (unless otherwise agreed), made any negotiated repairs, left behind all fixtures and other agreed-upon property, and left the place clean.

If you fail in one of your responsibilities, the buyer can use this as an excuse to delay the closing, bring up new repair or price requests (possibly getting a last-minute credit in escrow to make sure you take care of matters), or even cancel the sale. By now the buyer probably has the moving company all lined up and doesn't want delays any more than you do, but do your best to avoid sources of conflict.

A lot of sellers fall down on the job when it comes to final cleanup. You may be madly packing and moving into a new house yourself, and it's easy to forget a few boxes or a pile of trash in your old place. But wouldn't you be kicking yourself if the buyer made an issue of this? Take careful note of the final walk-through date, and make plans to have your house empty and spotless before that time.

Do your own final walk-through before the buyer does, looking for any repair issues that were previously hidden by your possessions. If, for example, some missing paint or plaster was hidden behind a bookshelf, or was created by your moving crew, do a quick touch-up. If you haven't been living in the house, make sure no new damage has occurred while you've been away, such as leaks or vandalism. These too are your responsibility to fix before the closing.

If you're going to be too exhausted for major scrubbing, arrange for a cleaning service to come in. You're expected to at least leave the place "broom clean"—in other words, not necessarily scrubbed or polished to a shine, but empty and swept clear of dirt or dust.

Dealing With Damage to the House During the Escrow Period

Until the closing day, you are the person with both legal title to and physical possession of the property, so you are responsible for maintaining its physical condition. If, for example, a fire damages the house three days before escrow closes, you are expected to either pay for repairs or get your insurance company to do so, and deliver the property in the condition it was in beforehand. Dealing with significant damage will, of course, probably take more than three days, meaning you'll have to ask the buyer for an extension of the closing date. A buyer who wants out of the deal may simply refuse to grant this extension.

What If You Need to Back Out of the Deal?

Your sale contract, as discussed in Chapter 9, probably gives you a few bases upon which to drop out of the deal, such as if you can't find another house to buy, or if the buyer fails to comply with a time limit or other obligation. If you back out for one of these reasons, there's no breach of contract, and the buyer has no grounds upon which to complain, much less sue for damages.

But, assuming the buyer has done everything set forth under the contract and removed all his or her contingencies, you can't back out of the deal just because you want to—most likely, because you've either changed your mind about selling (the house looked so good after all the repairs and staging!) or you've received another, higher offer. To back out now would be a clear breach of contract.

What would the buyer's remedy be? That, too, depends on your contract. Most likely, the buyer would need to demand that you mediate or arbitrate before actually suing you. The buyer might succeed in obtaining an order that you sell the house to him or her, and/or that you pay damages based on any out-of-pocket costs caused by your breach.

What If the Buyer Backs Out?

If the buyer tries to wiggle out of the deal without a reason that was contemplated within the contract, also look at your contract for how you can respond. Most likely you'd start by demanding mediation or arbitration, which might be followed by a lawsuit, requesting payment of damages. (You can't, ordinarily, force someone to complete the sale and buy your house.)

How high a damage payment you might receive depends on how easily you can turn around and sell the house to someone else—

which you are basically required to attempt, based on a legal duty to limit or mitigate damages. To avoid arguments over the exact amount of the loss, most house purchase contracts state that the buyer's earnest money payment becomes the maximum "liquidated damage" amount if the buyer breaches the contract.

Such disputes are often settled by the buyer agreeing to let the seller keep a portion, but not all, of the earnest money deposit. It's probably not worth a fight to keep every penny. Until you've settled this matter and are no longer in escrow with the first buyer, you're going to have trouble transferring clear title to the next buyer.

The Big Day: Your House Closing

Your wait is almost over. Here's what to expect on the closing day itself, when you'll exchange your house for the buyer's money. Whether you and the buyer meet face to face or conduct each of your halves of the transaction separately, the escrow agent will make sure that both of you feel safe handing over what you own to the other.

You'll likely have a "closing meeting" in the office of your escrow agent, attorney, or registrar of deeds. The choice of location depends mostly on local law or custom and who will be present. Your agent will probably be there, as well as the escrow agent, if there is one, and possibly your attorney, if you're represented. If you're meeting face to face with the buyer, his or her agent will also be there, and possibly the buyer's attorney. Nevertheless, because more and more can be handled electronically, the necessity for everyone to be in the room—or even in the same country—is greatly reduced.

RESOURCE

Download this checklist. You can download a copy of the Checklist of Items to Prepare for the Closing from Nolo.com. For instructions, see "Get Updates, Checklists, Calculators, and More at Nolo.com," in the Introduction.

Checklist of Items to Prepare for the Closing

Make sure you've got all of the below ready to bring to the closing table or transfer to the buyer:

- ☐ **Passport, driver's license, or other photo identification.** You may need to show it to the notary public who stamps the property deed or documents after you sign them.

- ☐ **Keys to your house.** The buyer will have trouble getting in without them!

- ☐ **Garage door opener.** Same issue.

- ☐ **House deed.** This will need to be turned over to the buyer, to transfer title. Your real estate agent will probably make sure this is taken care of, but talk to your escrow officer about whose responsibility it is if you're selling FSBO.

- ☐ **Home ownership records.** Closing is often the most logical time to hand over your product and appliance manuals and warranties, records of recent repairs, and names of repair people you've used and liked.

- ☐ **Utility payment records.** This means bringing receipts showing that you've paid the most recent water and sewer bills (which, if unpaid, can create liens on the property).

- ☐ **Any other required documents.** Your purchase contract may require you to deliver certain other items, such as condominium documents.

Keep in mind, on closing day, that you can't control everything. A lot has to come together simultaneously, and it's almost inevitable that something will go wrong, or some outstanding issue will remain unresolved. For example, Ngaire Taylor, a loan officer in Washington State, says, "I've seen condominium closings delayed because the condo association hadn't satisfied all the requirements set by the ultimate purchaser of the loan. Let's say the condo association needs to show that it has no greater than 15% delinquencies in dues collection.

That's not a situation where it can simply photocopy a document. The company might actually have to get busy collecting some of those dues, a process that might stretch right up to or past the closing date."

Fortunately, you'll be surrounded by a team of professionals, who've learned to deal with even the most difficult snafus. By now, the buyers have invested a lot of both time and money in buying the house. They're no more likely to walk away from the deal than you are.

> ⚠ **CAUTION**
>
> **Your buyer could still fail to qualify for a home loan.** "Some of the worst situations I've faced when representing home sellers," says Texas RE/MAX Realtor Greg Nino, "are when the buyers didn't realize that they couldn't just go out and buy a Mercedes and a bunch of furniture right before the closing and expect to qualify for the same loan that they were approved for a month or two ago. A misstep like that can delay or undo the deal right there." Unfortunately, meeting the financing contingency is something the buyer must, for the most part, handle without your input.

One of the biggest sources of closing snags is the buyer's lender, which must give final approval to the loan. No matter how much investigating the lender has done in the weeks leading up to the closing, it's not un-common for lenders to raise last-minute issues or make demands, such as for reconfirmation of the buyer's employment or photos proving that you really did install the required carbon monoxide detectors. Rest assured that a delayed closing doesn't necessarily mean the deal falls apart—it usually just means you're in suspense for a little longer.

> **Lesson learned the hard way** **Even the seller can get last-minute questions from the buyer's lender!** "I'd already fulfilled the mortgage company's request for a signed document stating that I wasn't married (thus showing that I had the power to sign the transfer deed on my own)," says Carter, after selling her Boston home. "But at the last minute, the mortgage company got nervous, and demanded that I prepare an actual sworn statement saying once again that I wasn't married. I complied, of course. But wouldn't you think that if someone were actually trying to commit a fraud, they'd try to perpetuate it on the sworn statement, too?"

When the deal is done, celebrate! You've made it through a challenging and often emotional process, and educated yourself so as to do it in the smartest way possible. Time to move on and start enjoying living in your next home. ●

Selling Without an Agent: Smart or Scary?

Your biggest home-selling expense is likely to be the fee you pay to your real estate agent: on average, 5% to 6% of the selling price. Even though in most cases it's eventually split with the buyer's agent, you, as the seller, pay the entire thing.

Would selling your home "by owner" (or FSBO, pronounced "fizz-bo"), without the help of a real estate professional, therefore save you money? That's a question that doesn't have a clear answer.

Plenty of statistics show that inexperienced sellers get lower prices than do experienced real estate agents, which then wipes out whatever savings they might have earned on the commission. But some common-sense arguments hold that, with home prices and therefore real estate agent commissions so high, even a seller who makes a few mistakes may come out ahead—particularly if the market is hot, and if that seller has made a careful study of the market and has the professional skills to market the property, negotiate the deal, and handle the paperwork involved in the sale (probably using a few hours of a lawyer's time).

Without knowing your local market and personal circumstances, we can't say whether or not selling FSBO would make sense for you. The people for whom it seems most logical are those who've already identified someone to whom they want to sell (perhaps a friend or family member), have settled on a price they're all happy with, and have the organizational and other skills needed to make sure the deal gets finalized in a legally appropriate fashion.

This chapter will explore these and other issues regarding selling on your own. We'll cover:

- the advantages and disadvantages of going FSBO
- whether you're likely to save money (this will depend on whether you pay the buyer's agent's commission, among other things), and
- important steps if you'll be marketing and advertising your FSBO.

TIP

How many people go FSBO? According to NAR's "2013 Profile of Home Buyers and Sellers," it's a mere 9% of home sellers. Of that group, 40% sold to someone they knew beforehand.

FSBO—The Way to Go?

Selling a home by owner offers potential advantages, including:

- **Reduced transaction costs.** The number one reason people sell on their own is to save the commission they'd otherwise pay to the real estate listing agent.
- **Competitive pricing.** If you're not paying a commission, you may be able to reduce your house's asking price, essentially "sharing" your savings with the buyer. This could bring in more prospective buyers. (But before you figure out how low to go, decide whether you plan to pay a commission to the buyer's agent, as discussed below.)

Do FSBO Sellers Save Money?

Ask any real estate agent and you're bound to hear that going FSBO is a near-fatal mistake. According to the National Association of Realtors, the average price of a house sold by owner in 2013 was $184,000, while the average sale price for an agent-sold home was $230,000. That's a large enough difference to more than make up for the agent's commission.

On the other side of the table, however, a 2008 study by *Consumer Reports* found that FSBO sellers get more for their homes—around $5,000 more, on average. And a 2012 study out of Stanford University found that a seller's use of a broker actually reduces the selling price of the typical home by 5.9% to 7.7%. So who's right?

It's hard to say—but if you want to sell FSBO and are willing to put the time and effort into handling the process well (including following the steps outlined in this chapter and book), you'll increase the chances that yours will be one of the FSBO sales that saves money.

- **Knowledge.** No one knows your house and neighborhood better than you do. You're in a fine position to impart that knowledge to a potential buyer.

There are disadvantages to selling FSBO, however. These include:

- **Lack of experience.** Unless you happen to be a real estate agent or attorney who's handled residential real estate matters, you won't have a significant knowledge base of the general home sales process, nor any experience with sales trends and customs in your geographic area. That may mean that you have to rely on (that is, pay) other professionals, and spend time educating yourself on some topics.

CAUTION

Don't let your lack of experience cost you. "I've seen FSBO sellers really alienate buyers, and that can risk deals," says Realtor Mark Nash. "For example, FSBO sellers who don't understand the home inspection process sometimes balk at perfectly reasonable requests by the buyers to make basic repairs in the $500 range. An agent would tell a seller with a good offer not to let something so minor jeopardize the deal. But unless the sellers understand the risks and see that making the repairs is the smartest move, they risk angering the buyer and potentially losing the deal."

- **Time and effort.** Selling on your own is a big time commitment. You'll have to do all the tasks a real estate agent would have handled. (For a review of these tasks, take a look at Chapter 2.) Not only will you have to learn how to price and market your property, you'll have to show it to interested buyers. When you do receive an offer, you'll have to evaluate it and handle all the paperwork associated with it.
- **Advertising challenges.** Many buyers today look for homes on the Internet, using various sites that draw primarily from the Multiple Listing Service (MLS) database. FSBO sellers can get their homes listed on the MLS (we'll explain how below), but it's often expensive. FSBO sellers will also have to take care of all other advertising (or pay a service that offers such support), such as photos, yard signs, open houses, and listing sheets. Distributing some of this material yourself may be harder without an agent since, unlike a professional agent, you won't be in constant contact with potential buyers and other agents.

- **Additional costs.** You may not save the entire 5% to 6% commission. After forking out cash for advertising, potentially paying a commission to the buyer's agent (as discussed below), and perhaps hiring an attorney to review your contract, you may find you're still paying out 3% or so.

Before deciding to go FSBO, weigh these pros and cons, and honestly consider whether you have the time, skill, knowledge, and perhaps most importantly, desire to get the job done—or to learn how to do it.

You should be highly motivated if you're selling FSBO, because you're your own salesperson. Your enthusiasm and perseverance will translate directly into how well you're able to generate interest in the property, thereby increasing the chances it will sell. Still interested? Keep reading.

Oops, the Buyer's Agent Wants a Commission!

Saving 5% to 6% sounds good, but would selling FSBO still be worthwhile if you saved only half that amount? You'll probably be faced with that question, for the simple reason that any prospective buyers who are using their own agent will need to find a way to pay that agent. And they're probably hoping you'll provide that payment—in real estate terms, you'll "cooperate."

You may think that paying a buyer's agent's commission defeats the purpose of selling FSBO in the first place—here you are trying to save money, only to pay an agent who is serving the buyer's, not your, needs. And if you're selling to someone you know, paying an agent a significant commission may seem particularly nonsensical, since one of the agent's primary tasks—matching the buyer to the seller—has already been taken care of.

Don't, however, automatically write off paying a cooperating commission. First of all, if you haven't yet found a buyer, a large part of marketing your property will involve getting the word out that it's for sale. Though the Internet is a fabulous tool for this, agents still play a significant role in matching buyers to sellers. And when agents know they won't get a commission from you, they're not motivated to show your listing to their prospective clients. They may discourage clients from looking at the place, or tell them horror stories of the difficulties of working directly with FSBO sellers who don't understand real estate customs and procedures. Letting agents know that you'll pay the cooperating commission keeps them motivated to show your home.

Also, involving a real estate agent means you won't be responsible for educating the buyer. While you'll need to do your own legwork to make the transaction successful, on the other side of the table will sit a professional who knows how the process works and who can provide the buyer with standard real estate forms and advice.

But don't assume paying the commission means the buyer's agent will educate *you*. It isn't the buyer's agent's responsibility to handle tasks your agent normally would. In fact, that's not what you want. As Realtor Nancy Atwood points out, "A buyer's agent has a fiduciary duty to represent the buyer's interests." If you're not willing to hire an agent of your own, Atwood advises, "The first thing you should do is hire a lawyer."

To save everyone time, decide whether you'll pay a cooperating commission ahead of time. If you announce your willingness up front, you won't get phone calls from agents asking if you'll pay the buyer's fee, and you can rest assured that agents will be more motivated to show your house to clients.

TIP

Don't pay twice. If you both lower your listing price to account for the full 5% to 6% commission *and* pay a buyers' agent, you'll lose out. If you're trying to attract buyers with a below-market list price, better to lower it by one or two percentage points and leave room to both pay a buyer's agent and compensate yourself for the efforts of selling FSBO.

Doing Your Own Marketing and Advertising

One of the most important steps in selling your property yourself is making sure that buyers know it's for sale (unless, of course, you've already found a buyer).

In Chapter 7, we cover some of the more general marketing strategies anyone can use to sell their home. Here, let's focus in on a few key tricks you'll need to know as a FSBO seller.

Be ready to spend some money on marketing—after all, if an agent were representing you, that's what he or she would be doing.

How Other FSBO Sellers Do Their Marketing

Here's what the other guy is doing by way of marketing—though perhaps that's not your best guide, given the statistics on how much less FSBO homes eventually sell for.

- Yard sign: 36%
- Friends, relatives, or neighbors: 28%
- Online classified advertisements: 16%
- Open house: 14%
- For-sale-by-owner websites: 13%
- Social networking websites (Facebook, Twitter, and so on): 7%
- Multiple Listing Service (MLS) website: 7%
- Print newspaper advertisement: 7%
- Direct mail (flyers, postcards, etc.): 1%
- Video: 1%
- Other: 2%.

In fact, around one third of FSBO sellers don't actively market their homes at all; but it's likely that these are the folks who decide to sell to a friend or family member.

Source: NAR "2013 Profile of Home Buyers and Sellers."

One of the first steps before posting your home online is to either hire a professional photographer or, if you've got photographic skills, take lots of pictures yourself. Do so on a sunny day when the house is clean and well presented (as described in Chapter 7). Take a panoply of shots, including as many rooms as the website or blog allows. Better yet, you might want to hire a pro to do a video or "virtual tour" of your home.

Marketing a FSBO Online

According to the National Association of Realtors, an overwhelming majority of prospective homebuyers look for properties online. And with the wealth of websites offering real estate listings, FSBOs are easier than ever for Internet-searching buyers to find. Still, it's worth posting your listing in various places.

Listing on the MLS

Most real estate agents list homes for sale on the Multiple Listing Service (MLS). Each MLS is a localized database of homes for sale in that area. Most MLS systems feed directly to www.realtor.com (the website for the National Association of Realtors). Some of the data also gets picked up by Zillow, Trulia, and other real estate websites.

Several online FSBO websites (discussed further below) will list your home on the MLS for a flat fee, usually a few hundred dollars. You might also be able to find an agent willing to list your property for a similar fee.

In Chapter 7, we explained more about what specific pieces of information to highlight in your MLS listing. As a FSBO seller, however, you should add to that list a mention of whether you're willing to pay a cooperating commission—the buyer's agent's commission discussed above—and if so, how much you'll pay.

Purchasing Services From a FSBO Website

Several online services offer advertising opportunities geared specifically to FSBO properties. Some of the more popular ones include www.forsalebyowner.com, www.byowner.com, www.owners.com, and www.fsbo.com.

On these and other sites, you can pay a relatively modest fee (beginning at less than $100) to list your home on that particular site and often slightly higher fees (up to around $1,000) for additional services, like a yard sign, a virtual tour, listing on the MLS, and color brochures or flyers.

> **TIP**
>
> **Peek at other FSBO listings for ideas on what works—or doesn't.** You will quickly notice things like, "Hey, this site gives lots of space for a property description—which makes that seller look really dumb for having entered only one long sentence (such as '2 bedrooms, 1 bathroom, big living room, fireplace, new paint inside and out, large yard, 2-car garage, near hospital and shopping'), rather than filling the space with details about the home."

Creating a Website or Blog Advertising Your Home

You can create online exposure for your home on your own, too. An easy way is to create a website or blog. One popular (and free) option is Postlets.com, which real estate agents also use. Owned by Zillow, it lets you create a property listing with a dedicated landing page on its site, then helps you distribute it to many other leading sites, such as Yahoo! Homes, HGTV/FrontDoor, and Craigslist.

Or, purchase a domain name at a website like www.godaddy.com or www.domain.com, which also help you set up and maintain your website. Many sellers purchase their home's address as a domain name—for example, www.950parkerstreet.com—and use this URL on promotional materials and yard signs.

Creating a blog is also easy, and can be free. Blogs tend to be easy to change, add to, or update, as well. Go to a publishing tool like www.blogger.com or www.wordpress.com; they'll walk you through the steps to create the blog and allow you to include both images and text.

As far as content, it's best to make sure your blog or website contains a lot of the same information as on your listing sheet. However, you have the opportunity to include more here. Pictures are probably the most important: Buyers go online to see which homes look interesting, and to avoid wasting their time visiting homes that don't match their wishes. If they're at all skeptical of a FSBO, posting one or two dark pictures that make the home look like it's owned by a recluse who won't let an agent walk in the door won't help matters.

TIP
Use social networking sites to promote your house. If you network with friends on sites like Facebook, Twitter, or Pinterest, don't forget to mention your home-selling plans, post photos, and link to your house's website or blog. You can also create a separate Facebook page for your listing—and thereby receive messages from those who view it—at https://apps.facebook.com/sellmyhousefast.

Should You Take Out a Classified Ad?

The traditional way to generate interest in a FSBO was to put a classified ad in your local newspaper. But today, it's probably not worth the effort or the cost. Buyers able to take full virtual tours online are less interested in 20-word descriptions full of cryptic abbreviations.

That said, an online classified ad through your local—that is, small city or neighborhood—newspaper may be cheap and effective. Be sure to include the property's Web address in the listing so that buyers can have a look for themselves.

Posting Signs

One good, old-fashioned way to get the word out that your house is for sale is to post a sign in your front yard. While picking up a simple "For Sale" sign at your local hardware store is probably the cheapest option (short of scrawling the words on a piece of cardboard), it's also likely to be the least effective. The information you write on the sign, such as your contact information or the list price, will be too small for anyone driving by to read. A small, cheap sign doesn't look very professional, either—which telegraphs to buyers that your home itself may be cheap or tacky.

Instead, have a sturdy, high-quality sign made that you can put close to the road, allowing anyone driving or walking by to see it clearly. The sign should include a phone number where prospective buyers can reach you. You may even consider designating a phone line to provide prerecorded information about the house to interested buyers.

While you're ordering signs, you may also want to buy some "Open House" signs (as discussed below).

CAUTION

Don't be surprised by a knock on the door. Some interested buyers think that selling FSBO means you're willing to take personal inquiries at any time. If someone walking by knocks and you choose to open the door, try to schedule a time for a showing.

FSBO websites typically offer packages that include a yard sign. If you buy one of these, you'll want to know whether the sign comes with any "riders"—those extra templates that hang off the primary sign in order to convey extra information, such as "Open Sunday 1-4." You will also want to know whether you'll get a flyer box: that's the small box, often mounted on the sign post, that provides printed flyers to interested parties. If your sign will have a flyer box, keep it well stocked—we'll explain what to put on the flyer in the next section.

Creating a Listing Sheet

A flyer or "listing sheet" can be a useful and multifunctional marketing tool. You can put it out with your yard sign, distribute it at open houses or when you give tours, or send it to neighbors (who might spread the word to their friends).

Your goal with a listing sheet is twofold: to give the buyer a little information about the place and to make it attractive and memorable so the prospective buyer will either visit it or remember it after a visit. But you don't want to overwhelm readers with information. To make your flyer stand out:

- **Use a header.** In a font larger than the rest of the text, catch the buyer's eye with a descriptive and intriguing heading, such as "Picture-Perfect Starter in Desirable Heritage Park."

- **Include photos.** At the very least, you'll need a picture of the home's exterior. If you can add a flattering, perhaps smaller, indoor shot or two, even better.

- **Keep it short.** Describe the basics—the number of bedrooms, bathrooms, square feet, when the house was built, and so forth. You might use bullet points to convey this information, but don't drone on and on—the flyer will look busy, and you won't leave any mystery.

- **Be descriptive.** Mention the home's best features, such as "refinished hardwood floors throughout and kitchen fully remodeled in 2012." Focus on elements that will capture a buyer's interest, such as the environmentally friendly solar panels and tankless water heater, the luxurious master suite, or the fully landscaped backyard paradise.

- **Make it readable.** Don't try to jam text into too small a space, like with an eight-point font. Buyers won't be able to read it and will lose interest.

- **Highlight your contact information.** Make it easy for a prospective buyer to reach you. Don't put your home phone number on the sheet if you really only use your cell phone. Then again, don't put your cell phone number down if you're not willing to take calls pretty much any time of day. For buyers who are curious but maybe not ready to talk to you, include your Web or blog address.

Holding Open Houses

If you were to hire an agent, he or she would likely conduct one or two open houses. Should you do the same? While open houses may attract more curious neighbors than serious buyers, they can be important for creating publicity that you might not otherwise get. After all, local agents who represent buyers may not even know your property is for sale, or in the worst case, may try to discourage prospective buyers from looking at it, especially if you don't offer to pay the cooperating commission. An open house creates activity around your property and heightens its visibility.

Responding to Agents Who Want to Represent You

As a FSBO seller, you'll probably be approached by at least one real estate agent looking to help take the property off your hands by listing it with him or her. If so, you needn't necessarily dismiss the offer out of hand. (And if you're willing to pay a cooperating commission if the agent brings you a buyer, point that out.)

If the agent tries to convince you that he or she will be able to help you sell the home, ask for specifics on how these marketing efforts will work better than your own. Don't be afraid to stick to your guns—if you change your mind later, you'll have no trouble finding an agent to work with.

If an agent claims to have an interested buyer, be receptive but cautious. Some agents don't have any specific buyer or may have several they'd show your property to, but are really just looking for another way to get you to list your property with them. Invite the agent to bring the buyer on a home tour, but don't waste a lot of time on the phone discussing the particulars. And keep in mind that anything you disclose to the agent is likely to get back to the prospective buyer or buyers.

If an agent were listing your home, he or she would probably politely ask you to clear out of the house during the open house. There's a good reason for this. It's hard to hear criticisms about the color of your bedroom walls or the kitchen remodel you so lovingly slaved over. And unlike you, an agent is trained not to seem too eager (which can seem desperate or invasive) when a prospective buyer shows interest, or to start over-sharing.

When selling your house FSBO, however, you won't have an agent to act as a buffer. That means you'll have to keep cool and temper any natural defensive or hovering instincts when doing your open houses.

So, get ready to conduct your own open house and maybe more than one. Your job at an open house is to be a salesperson—to acquaint prospective buyers with your home's many amenities, without laying it on too thick. Here are some tips for doing this:

- **Set your open house for a convenient time.** Open houses traditionally occur on weekends, and last for at least a couple hours. If you're used to seeing open houses at certain times in your neighborhood—for example, 1–4 on a Sunday—you may also increase traffic by starting a little earlier and running a little later (such as 12–5). Another way to increase traffic is to choose an additional, but also convenient time—perhaps a weekday evening.

- **Set out several open-house signs.** In addition to your regular yard sign, you may want to purchase one or more "directional" signs that tell prospective buyers where to go. Place these at busy intersections near your house, and one right in front.

- **Welcome looky-loos.** You're sure to get neighbors who are just curious about what's for sale in the neighborhood and at what price. Instead of dismissing or being suspicious of such neighbors, welcome them. You never know who they know— perhaps they'll tell friends or relatives who are looking to buy. In fact, you might put out snacks to create a festive atmosphere.

- **Ask visitors to sign in.** This serves more than one purpose. First, it protects you—if you're going to open your home, you have a right to know who's in it. But it also gives you an opportunity to follow up. For example, you can call someone who seemed interested, ask whether they've had an opportunity to think about it, and offer to show them the place again.

- **Provide marketing material.** Make sure you've got plenty of copies of your listing sheet or other marketing material ready to hand out, so interested buyers can walk away with something. Have copies of inspection reports or your disclosure statement ready for buyers who ask for them, as well.

- **Show visitors around.** This not only allows you to highlight your home's lovely features, it protects you. Occasionally, open houses are visited by people who have no interest in buying homes, but are instead planning to scope them out and help themselves to things they find. You can protect yourself by carefully storing your valuables and medicines, and keeping an eye on who's where. Watch out for the old trick of one person engaging you in an intense conversation while the other one roams your house alone. (It may take more than one person to deal with multiple visitors, so enlist the help of a partner or friend, if necessary.)

- **Get the kids and pets out.** You're sure to be distracted if you have little ones—or furry ones—running around. And both take away from a buyer's ability to see themselves living in the home.

- **Dress appropriately.** You're not having friends over for a weekend barbeque. This is a professional transaction, so dress the part—a full suit probably isn't necessary, but business-casual attire shows you're to be taken seriously.

- **Make your home look great.** Follow the advice in Chapters 3 and 5 to ensure the property is in good shape before you throw open your doors.

Showing Your House

In addition to open houses, you'll be responsible for showing your house to interested buyers by appointment—sometimes more than once. Making sure the house is in tip-top shape for each viewing takes enough time as it is, but it's only the beginning if you're a FSBO seller.

The main challenge with showing your house yourself is that it's easy to come on too strong. While you're motivated to sell the place, you don't want the prospective buyer to feel like there's a salesperson crawling down his or her throat, trying to explain away any problems with the house and insist that it's worth buying.

At the same time, you don't want to reveal too much. For example, if a prospective buyer asks you why you're moving, don't launch into a discussion about the great new job you're starting in a week, in a city across the country. You don't want to divulge any clues about how desperate you are to sell or how low a price you'd be willing to accept.

It's best to treat the visit like an individual open house—an opportunity to show the place off to someone whom you hope, but don't assume, may become interested in buying the place.

Plan to walk through each room together. Offer general information about the room, such as "This is the only bedroom on this floor; the floors were refinished two years ago," but don't provide an exhaustive list of every physical detail or how you've spent your time there—that's the last thing the buyer wants to hear.

While you allow buyers to enter a room and look around, don't follow right on their heels. Instead, hang back around the doorway. Make sure they know you're available to answer any questions (and make sure you know the answers to the most basic ones, like when remodeling projects were completed). Allow the buyer some quiet time to look without listening to you.

When prospective buyers are ready to leave, remind them how to contact you with any questions. Also double-check that you have their contact information. You may want to follow up in a few days, just to see if they have any additional questions.

CAUTION

Think twice before letting visitors in when you're not home. FSBO websites offer sellers lockboxes similar to those used by realtors, with which you can give prospective visitors access to your home. If the prospective buyers are represented by a real estate agent with local standing, you can probably rely on that person's professionalism—they enter sellers' homes all the time to do showings. But if not, and the prospective buyer isn't a friend or family member, this seems like a bad idea.

Receiving an Offer and Negotiating a FSBO Deal

After all your hard work, you'll be thrilled if and when you finally get an offer. But don't celebrate just yet. Many real estate offers never make it to sales. And even if they do, there are lots of other steps first. The top challenge reported by FSBO sellers (in NAR's "2013 Profile of Buyers and Sellers") was understanding and completing paperwork, so this is where you'll want to buckle down and do your homework or get a lawyer involved early on.

To understand the terms of any offer you receive and how to negotiate the sale, start by reading Chapter 8. Here, we're simply going to talk about three key issues unique to FSBO offers: how to handle negotiations in person, comply with your legal obligations, and get the help you need to close the deal.

TIP

Is the buyer really going to be able to pay for the house? It doesn't do much good to accept an offer and negotiate a deal only to find out that the buyer doesn't have a sufficiently large down payment or can't get a mortgage to buy the place. As a FSBO seller, one of your most important tasks when reviewing an offer—particularly if the buyer is unrepresented—is to examine the buyer's financial situation. See details on how to do that in Chapter 8.

Negotiating With the Buyer

Negotiating successfully is a skill, and one of the reasons many people choose an agent in the first place. You and the buyer have two very different objectives: You want to sell the house for as much as you can, and the buyer wants to buy it for as little as possible. You can take a hardline approach: "I won't take a penny less than my asking price!" or "I need at least 60 days to complete this sale and move out!" But it's less likely to keep the buyer's interest.

In most states, reaching an agreement doesn't normally involve sitting down and hashing things out with a buyer, however. That's because the real estate industry has developed a more formalized means of negotiation, in which the seller and the buyer, usually through their agents, exchange written offers and counteroffers, perhaps with a formal, in-person meeting at the very beginning.

Exactly how that's done is a matter of local custom. Sellers and buyers don't literally have to send or deliver original documents via U.S. mail—it's become normal to exchange email attachments and then later follow up with the original. If you expect multiple offers, you might set a date and time by which you must receive them.

On the other hand, if you find it easier, there's nothing to stop you and the buyer from sitting down at a table together and going over the details until you've reached a solid agreement. How comfortable you feel with the buyer may also play into this decision. If you end up selling to a good friend or the neighbor whom you've met at social events, it may be easier and more comfortable to get together—even in the house—to work out the deal. Just make sure you don't get so lulled into a sense of comfort and complacency that you start making concessions you wouldn't otherwise make.

The last step in your negotiations is for you and the buyer to sign the purchase contract. No matter who goes first in drafting the contract, you aren't "in contract" until both of you have signed. See Chapters 8 and 9 for an analysis of what goes into the purchase contract, including which terms are or aren't worth negotiating hard over.

TIP
Review blank documents ahead of time. It's a good idea to review a blank offer, contract, disclosures, and other forms—if you're using a standard set—before you begin any negotiations. You won't have someone there representing your interests, so you need to hit the ground running.

Although we recommend getting familiar with the documents, it really is best to hire an attorney to assist you in finalizing the transaction (as is required in many states in any case). This is likely to cost several hundred dollars. In addition to helping you understand the standard forms, your attorney can inform you about any special contract requirements in your state, plus review the completed agreement with you. In some states, a title officer may be able to provide you with copies of standard documents—but don't expect much else, as it's not the title officer's job to educate or represent you.

Complying With Your Legal Obligations

If you don't hire an attorney at the beginning of the process, or you aren't using an online FSBO-facilitation service, you'll need to take extra steps to make sure you comply with all applicable real estate rules and regulations.

First and foremost, your state's law probably mandates that you fill out a complete set of disclosure documents, as described in Chapter 4. Get these ready well in advance of showing your home to buyers. After having taken a careful look at the issues and defects in your home, you may even decide to lower your list price. And even if your state doesn't have a disclosure law, federal law imposes certain disclosure requirements, also discussed in Chapter 4.

Your state's department or commission of real estate or related government agency should be able to alert you to any other local laws relevant to home sellers. A simple Internet search will turn up the department's website. For example, the Minnesota Attorney General's office provides an online "Home Sellers Handbook," and the Massachusetts Office of Consumer Affairs & Business Regulation devotes a Web page to "Buying and selling a home in Massachusetts."

If you live in a community governed by a homeowners' association (HOA), additional rules may apply to your home sale. Read your CC&Rs and other governing documents and get in touch with the HOA about your plans as soon as possible. You'll need to find out about issues like what happens if you leave the house vacant while you're selling it, and what transfer fees you may need to pay to the HOA.

Closing the Deal

Your purchase contract is an important legal document, signifying that neither you nor the buyer can back out of the sale without a valid reason. But signing the contract doesn't seal the deal—there's more work to be done first. For one, the contract will doubtless contain several "contingencies," based upon which either you or the buyer can cancel the deal if certain criteria aren't met. For example, if your contract has an inspection contingency, the buyer can conduct an inspection and condition the sale on approving the results—or use these results to negotiate for changes in the terms of the deal.

And that's just the beginning, as you may remember from when you bought the home. We discuss more of this in Chapter 10, but the bottom line is that the deal isn't over until weeks after the purchase contract is signed, when the sale has formally closed and the deed has been recorded. Although the buyer will be doing a lot of the work—coordinating inspections, lining up financing, and so forth—you'll want to make sure the buyer is meeting any deadlines outlined in your agreement.

You may have your own contingencies and requirements to meet, as well. For example, you may have included a contingency that you enter into contract to purchase another home before selling this one (something the buyer will likely only agree to in a super-hot market). Or, if you live in a home governed by a community association, you will likely need to obtain a clearance letter and/or compliance certificate from your homeowners' association saying that you don't owe any outstanding fees or dues, and that the current condition of your property doesn't violate any association rules.

Fortunately, you won't need to handle all of this alone—you'll hire a neutral third party, either an escrow or title agent (this person's name and role depends on what state you live in) or an attorney to organize and orchestrate many of the details and make sure you and the buyer both do what you're supposed to do by the closing date. If you were happy with the closing or escrow company that helped you buy the house, that may be the first place to go for help in selling it. Or, ask friends or local Realtors for recommendations.

TIP

It's a good idea to choose the closing agent well in advance of signing the purchase contract. That way, that you'll know which attorney or company to list on the contract, and can ask about any special requirements or rules in your state.

Also, as we explained above, because you may be responsible for some duties that come with serious legal consequences—for example, preparing the deed or making sure title is clear—you may want an attorney to ensure you handle everything correctly. (Hiring one to review your work can be significantly cheaper than hiring one to do the work from scratch, though not all attorneys will agree to such an arrangement.) If you're in a state where title companies handle escrow, the title agent may do some of this. ●

Index

⚖ NOLO *Online Legal Forms*

Nolo offers a large library of legal solutions and forms, created by Nolo's in-house legal staff. These reliable documents can be prepared in minutes.

Create a Document

- **Incorporation.** Incorporate your business in any state.
- **LLC Formations.** Gain asset protection and pass-through tax status in any state.
- **Wills.** Nolo has helped people make over 2 million wills. Is it time to make or revise yours?
- **Living Trust (avoid probate).** Plan now to save your family the cost, delays, and hassle of probate.
- **Trademark.** Protect the name of your business or product.
- **Provisional Patent.** Preserve your rights under patent law and claim "patent pending" status.

Download a Legal Form

Nolo.com has hundreds of top quality legal forms available for download—bills of sale, promissory notes, nondisclosure agreements, LLC operating agreements, corporate minutes, commercial lease and sublease, motor vehicle bill of sale, consignment agreements and many more.

Review Your Documents

Many lawyers in Nolo's consumer-friendly lawyer directory will review Nolo documents for a very reasonable fee. Check their detailed profiles at **Nolo.com/lawyers**.

Nolo's Bestselling Books

101 Law Forms for Personal Use
$29.99

Neighbor Law
Fences, Trees, Boundaries & Noise
$29.99

Every Landlord's Legal Guide
$44.99

Get It Together
Organize Your Records So Your Family Won't Have To
$24.99

The Legal Answer Book for Families
$24.99

Every Nolo title is available in print and for download at Nolo.com.